Wei Wei, MA, MLS
Sue O'Neill Johnson, BA, MLS, MPA
Sylvia E. A. Piggott, BA, MLS
Editors

Leadership and Management Principles in Libraries in Developing Countries

Leadership and Management Principles in Libraries in Developing Countries has been co-published simultaneously as *Science & Technology Libraries*, Volume 23, Numbers 2/3 2002.

Pre-publication
REVIEWS,
COMMENTARIES,
EVALUATIONS . . .

" A FASCINATING READ that transports you into the everyday reality of practicing librarianship in a developing country. The energy, leadership, and innovative ideas of the authors are inspiring. For those of us in developed countries who take Internet connectivity and adequate library facilities for granted, this book is a refreshing reminder that challenges in information science come in all shapes and sizes. It helps illustrate how librarians internationally can learn from each other."

G. Lynn Berard, AMLS
Head, Science Libraries
Carnegie Mellon University

 **Routledge**
Taylor & Francis Group

LONDON AND NEW YORK

Leadership
and Management
Principles in Libraries
in Developing Countries

Leadership and Management Principles in Libraries in Developing Countries has been co-published simultaneously as *Science & Technology Libraries*, Volume 23, Numbers 2/3 2002.

Science & Technology Libraries Monographic "Separates"

Below is a list of "separates," which in serials librarianship means a special issue simultaneously published as a special journal issue or double-issue *and* as a "separate" hardbound monograph. (This is a format which we also call a "DocuSerial.")

"Separates" are published because specialized libraries or professionals may wish to purchase a specific thematic issue by itself in a format which can be separately cataloged and shelved, as opposed to purchasing the journal on an on-going basis. Faculty members may also more easily consider a "separate" for classroom adoption.

"Separates" are carefully classified separately with the major book jobbers so that the journal tie-in can be noted on new book order slips to avoid duplicate purchasing.

You may wish to visit Haworth's website at . . .

http://www.HaworthPress.com

. . . to search our online catalog for complete tables of contents of these separates and related publications.

You may also call 1-800-HAWORTH (outside US/Canada: 607-722-5857), or Fax: 1-800-895-0582 (outside US/Canada: 607-771-0012), or e-mail at:

docdelivery@haworthpress.com

Digital Libraries: Philosophies, Technical Design Considerations, and Example Scenarios, edited by David Stern (Vol. 17, No. 3/4, 1999). *"Digital Libraries: Philosophies, Technical Design Considerations, and Example Scenarios targets the general librarian population and does a good job of opening eyes to the impact that digital library projects are already having in our automated libraries." (Kimberly J. Parker, MILS, Electronic Publishing & Collections Librarian, Yale University Library)*

Sci/Tech Librarianship: Education and Training, edited by Julie Hallmark, PhD, and Ruth K. Seidman, MSLS (Vol. 17, No. 2, 1998). *"Insightful, informative, and right-on-the-mark. . . . This collection provides a much-needed view of the education of sci/tech librarians." (Michael R. Leach, AB, Director, Physics Research Library, Harvard University)*

Chemical Librarianship: Challenges and Opportunities, edited by Arleen N. Somerville (Vol. 16, No. 3/4, 1997). *"Presents a most satisfying collection of articles that will be of interest, first and foremost, to chemistry librarians, but also to science librarians working in other science disciplines within academic settings." (Barbara List, Director, Science and Engineering Libraries, Columbia University, New York, New York)*

History of Science and Technology: A Sampler of Centers and Collections of Distinction, edited by Cynthia Steinke, MS (Vol. 14, No. 4, 1995). *"A 'grand tour' of history of science and technology collections that is of great interest to scholars, students and librarians." (Jay K. Lucker, AB, MSLS, Director of Libraries, Massachusetts Institute of Technology; Lecturer in Science and Technology, Simmons College, Graduate School of Library and Information Science)*

Instruction for Information Access in Sci-Tech Libraries, edited by Cynthia Steinke, MS (Vol. 14, No. 2, 1994). *"A refreshing mix of user education programs and contain[s] many examples of good practice." (Library Review and Reference Reviews)*

Scientific and Clinical Literature for the Decade of the Brain, edited by Tony Stankus, MLS (Vol. 13, No. 3/4, 1993). *"This format combined with selected book and journal title lists is very convenient for life science, social science, or general reference librarians/bibliographers who wish to review the area or get up to speed quickly." (Ruth Lewis, MLS, Biology Librarian, Washington University, St. Louis, Missouri)*

Sci-Tech Libraries of the Future, edited by Cynthia Steinke, MS (Vol. 12, No. 4 and Vol. 13, No. 1, 1993). *"Very timely. . . . Will be of interest to all libraries confronted with changes in technology, information formats, and user expectations." (LA Record)*

Science Librarianship at America's Liberal Arts Colleges: Working Librarians Tell Their Stories, edited by Tony Stankus, MLS (Vol. 12, No. 3, 1992). *"For those teetering on the tightrope between the needs and desires of science faculty and liberal arts librarianship, this book brings a sense of balance." (Teresa R. Faust, MLS, Science Reference Librarian, Wake Forest University)*

Biographies of Scientists for Sci-Tech Libraries: Adding Faces to the Facts, edited by Tony Stankus, MLS (Vol. 11, No. 4, 1992). *"A guide to biographies of scientists from a wide variety of scientific fields, identifying titles that reveal the personality of the biographee as well as contributions to his/her field." (Sci Tech Book News)*

Information Seeking and Communicating Behavior of Scientists and Engineers, edited by Cynthia Steinke, MS (Vol. 11, No. 3, 1991). *"Unequivocally recommended. . . . The subject is one of importance to most university libraries, which are actively engaged in addressing user needs as a framework for library services." (New Library World)*

Technology Transfer: The Role of the Sci-Tech Librarian, edited by Cynthia Steinke, MS (Vol. 11, No. 2, 1991). *"Educates the reader about the role of information professionals in the multifaceted technology transfer process." (Journal of Chemical Information and Computer Sciences)*

Electronic Information Systems in Sci-Tech Libraries, edited by Cynthia Steinke, MS (Vol. 11, No. 1, 1990). *"Serves to illustrate the possibilities for effective networking from any library/information facility to any other geographical point." (Library Journal)*

The Role of Trade Literature in Sci-Tech Libraries, edited by Ellis Mount, DLS (Vol. 10, No. 4, 1990). *"A highly useful resource to identify and discuss the subject of manufacturers' catalogs and their historical as well as practical value to the profession of librarianship. Dr. Mount has made an outstanding contribution." (Academic Library Book Review)*

Role of Standards in Sci-Tech Libraries, edited by Ellis Mount, DLS (Vol. 10, No. 3, 1990). *Required reading for any librarian who has been asked to identify standards and specifications.*

Relation of Sci-Tech Information to Environmental Studies, edited by Ellis Mount, DLS (Vol. 10, No. 2, 1990). *"A timely and important book that illustrates the nature and use of sci-tech information in relation to the environment." (The Bulletin of Science, Technology & Society)*

End-User Training for Sci-Tech Databases, edited by Ellis Mount, DLS (Vol. 10, No. 1, 1990). *"This is a timely publication for those of us involved in conducting online searches in special libraries where our users have a detailed knowledge of their subject areas." (Australian Library Review)*

Sci-Tech Archives and Manuscript Collections, edited by Ellis Mount, DLS (Vol. 9, No. 4, 1989). *Gain valuable information on the ways in which sci-tech archival material is being handled and preserved in various institutions and organizations.*

Collection Management in Sci-Tech Libraries, edited by Ellis Mount, DLS (Vol. 9, No. 3, 1989). *"An interesting and timely survey of current issues in collection management as they pertain to science and technology libraries." (Barbara A. List, AMLS, Coordinator of Collection Development, Science & Technology Research Center, and Editor, New Technical Books, The Research Libraries, New York Public Library)*

The Role of Conference Literature in Sci-Tech Libraries, edited by Ellis Mount, DLS (Vol. 9, No. 2, 1989). *"The volume constitutes a valuable overview of the issues posed for librarians and users by one of the most frustrating and yet important sources of scientific and technical information." (Australian Library Review)*

Adaptation of Turnkey Computer Systems in Sci-Tech Libraries, edited by Ellis Mount, DLS (Vol. 9, No. 1, 1989). *"Interesting and useful. . . . The book addresses the problems and benefits associated with the installation of a turnkey or ready-made computer system in a scientific or technical library." (Information Retrieval & Library Automation)*

Sci-Tech Libraries Serving Zoological Gardens, edited by Ellis Mount, DLS (Vol. 8, No. 4, 1989). *"Reviews the history and development of six major zoological garden libraries in the U.S." (Australian Library Review)*

Libraries Serving Science-Oriented and Vocational High Schools, edited by Ellis Mount, DLS (Vol. 8, No. 3, 1989). *A wealth of information on the special collections of science-oriented and vocational high schools, with a look at their services, students, activities, and problems.*

Sci-Tech Library Networks Within Organizations, edited by Ellis Mount, DLS (Vol. 8, No. 2, 1988). *Offers thorough descriptions of sci-tech library networks in which their members have a common sponsorship or ownership.*

One Hundred Years of Sci-Tech Libraries: A Brief History, edited by Ellis Mount, DLS (Vol. 8, No. 1, 1988). *"Should be read by all those considering, or who are already involved in, information retrieval, whether in Sci-tech libraries or others." (Library Resources & Technical Services)*

Alternative Careers in Sci-Tech Information Service, edited by Ellis Mount, DLS (Vol. 7, No. 4, 1987). *Here is an eye-opening look at alternative careers for professionals with a sci-tech background, including librarians, scientists, and engineers.*

Preservation and Conservation of Sci-Tech Materials, edited by Ellis Mount, DLS (Vol. 7, No. 3, 1987). *"This cleverly coordinated work is essential reading for library school students and practicing librarians. . . . Recommended reading." (Science Books and Films)*

Sci-Tech Libraries Serving Societies and Institutions, edited by Ellis Mount, DLS (Vol. 7, No. 2, 1987). *"Of most interest to special librarians, providing them with some insight into sci-tech libraries and their activities as well as a means of identifying specialized services and collections which may be of use to them." (Sci-Tech Libraries)*

Innovations in Planning Facilities for Sci-Tech Libraries, edited by Ellis Mount, DLS (Vol. 7, No. 1, 1986). *"Will prove invaluable to any librarian establishing a new library or contemplating expansion." (Australasian College Libraries)*

Role of Computers in Sci-Tech Libraries, edited by Ellis Mount, DLS (Vol. 6, No. 4, 1986). *"A very readable text. . . . I am including a number of the articles in the student reading list." (C. Bull, Kingstec Community College, Kentville, Nova Scotia, Canada)*

Weeding of Collections in Sci-Tech Libraries, edited by Ellis Mount, DLS (Vol. 6, No. 3, 1986). *"A useful publication. . . . Should be in every science and technology library." (Rivernia Library Review)*

Sci-Tech Libraries in Museums and Aquariums, edited by Ellis Mount, DLS (Vol. 6, No. 1/2, 1985). *"Useful to libraries in museums and aquariums for its descriptive and practical information." (The Association for Information Management)*

Data Manipulation in Sci-Tech Libraries, edited by Ellis Mount, DLS (Vol. 5, No. 4, 1985). *"Papers in this volume present evidence of the growing sophistication in the manipulation of data by information personnel." (Sci-Tech Book News)*

Role of Maps in Sci-Tech Libraries, edited by Ellis Mount, DLS (Vol. 5, No. 3, 1985). *Learn all about the acquisition of maps and the special problems of their storage and preservation in this insightful book.*

Fee-Based Services in Sci-Tech Libraries, edited by Ellis Mount, DLS (Vol. 5, No. 2, 1985). *"Highly recommended. Any librarian will find something of interest in this volume." (Australasian College Libraries)*

Serving End-Users in Sci-Tech Libraries, edited by Ellis Mount, DLS (Vol. 5, No. 1, 1984). *"Welcome and indeed interesting reading. . . . a useful acquisition for anyone starting out in one or more of the areas covered." (Australasian College Libraries)*

Management of Sci-Tech Libraries, edited by Ellis Mount, DLS (Vol. 4, No. 3/4, 1984). *Become better equipped to tackle difficult staffing, budgeting, and personnel challenges with this essential volume on managing different types of sci-tech libraries.*

Collection Development in Sci-Tech Libraries, edited by Ellis Mount, DLS (Vol. 4, No. 2, 1984). *"Well-written by authors who work in the field they are discussing. Should be of value to librarians whose collections cover a wide range of scientific and technical fields." (Library Acquisitions: Practice and Theory)*

Role of Serials in Sci-Tech Libraries, edited by Ellis Mount, DLS (Vol. 4, No. 1, 1983). *"Some interesting nuggets to offer dedicated serials librarians and users of scientific journal literature. . . . Outlines the direction of some major changes already occurring in scientific journal publishing and serials management." (Serials Review)*

Planning Facilities for Sci-Tech Libraries, edited by Ellis Mount, DLS (Vol. 3, No. 4, 1983). *"Will be of interest to special librarians who are contemplating the building of new facilities or the renovating and adaptation of existing facilities in the near future. . . . A useful manual based on actual experiences." (Sci-Tech News)*

Monographs in Sci-Tech Libraries, edited by Ellis Mount, DLS (Vol. 3, No. 3, 1983). *This insightful book addresses the present contributions monographs are making in sci-tech libraries as well as their probable role in the future.*

Role of Translations in Sci-Tech Libraries, edited by Ellis Mount, DLS (Vol. 3, No. 2, 1983). *"Good required reading in a course on special libraries in library school. It would also be useful to any librarian who handles the ordering of translations." (Sci-Tech News)*

Online versus Manual Searching in Sci-Tech Libraries, edited by Ellis Mount, DLS (Vol. 3, No. 1, 1982). *An authoritative volume that examines the role that manual searches play in academic, public, corporate, and hospital libraries.*

Document Delivery for Sci-Tech Libraries, edited by Ellis Mount, DLS (Vol. 2, No. 4, 1982). *Touches on important aspects of document delivery and the place each aspect holds in the overall scheme of things.*

Cataloging and Indexing for Sci-Tech Libraries, edited by Ellis Mount, DLS (Vol. 2, No. 3, 1982). *Diverse and authoritative views on the problems of cataloging and indexing in sci-tech libraries.*

Role of Patents in Sci-Tech Libraries, edited by Ellis Mount, DLS (Vol. 2, No. 2, 1982). *A fascinating look at the nature of patents and the complicated, ever-changing set of indexes and computerized databases devoted to facilitating the identification and retrieval of patents.*

Current Awareness Services in Sci-Tech Libraries, edited by Ellis Mount, DLS (Vol. 2, No. 1, 1982). *An interesting and comprehensive look at the many forms of current awareness services that sci-tech libraries offer.*

Role of Technical Reports in Sci-Tech Libraries, edited by Ellis Mount, DLS (Vol. 1, No. 4, 1982). *Recommended reading not only for science and technology librarians, this unique volume is specifically devoted to the analysis of problems, innovative practices, and advances relating to the control and servicing of technical reports.*

Training of Sci-Tech Librarians and Library Users, edited by Ellis Mount, DLS (Vol. 1, No. 3, 1981). *Here is a crucial overview of the current and future issues in the training of science and engineering librarians as well as instruction for users of these libraries.*

Networking in Sci-Tech Libraries and Information Centers, edited by Ellis Mount, DLS (Vol. 1, No. 2, 1981). *Here is an entire volume devoted to the topic of cooperative projects and library networks among sci-tech libraries.*

Planning for Online Search Service in Sci-Tech Libraries, edited by Ellis Mount, DLS (Vol. 1, No. 1, 1981). *Covers the most important issue to consider when planning for online search services.*

Leadership and Management Principles in Libraries in Developing Countries

Wei Wei
Sue O'Neill Johnson
Sylvia E. A. Piggott
Editors

Leadership and Management Principles in Libraries in Developing Countries has been co-published simultaneously as *Science & Technology Libraries*, Volume 23, Numbers 2/3 2002.

Taylor & Francis Group

LONDON AND NEW YORK

Leadership and Management Principles in Libraries in Developing Countries has been co-published simultaneously as *Science & Technology Libraries*™, Volume 23, Numbers 2/3 2002.

First published 2002 by The Haworth Press, Inc.

2 Park Square, Milton Park, Abingdon, Oxfordshire OX14 4RN
605 Third Avenue, New York, NY 10017

Routledge is an imprint of the Taylor & Francis Group, an informa business

First issued in hardback 2020

Cover design by Jennifer M. Gaska.

Library of Congress Cataloging-in-Publication Data

Leadership and management principles in libraries in developing countries / Wei Wei, Sue O'Neill Johnson, Sylvia E. A. Piggott, editors.
     p. cm.
     Papers selected from those submitted to the Special Libraries Association, Leadership and Management Division's 2003 International Paper Competition.
     "Co-published simultaneously as Science & technology libraries, volume 23, numbers 2/3."
     Includes bibliographical references and index.
     ISBN 0-7890-2410-1 (alk. paper) – ISBN 0-7890-2411-X (pbk. : alk.paper)
     1. Libraries–Developing countries. 2. Library administration–Developing countries. 3. Special libraries–Developing countries. 4. Information services–Developing countries. I. Wei, Wei, 1952- II. Johnson, Sue O'Neill. III. Piggott, Sylvia E. A. IV. Science & technology libraries.
Z730.L43 2004
027.0172'4–dc22
                                                    2003021694

ISBN 978-0-7890-2410-7 (hbk)

Indexing, Abstracting & Website/Internet Coverage

Science & Technology Libraries

This section provides you with a list of major indexing & abstracting services. That is to say, each service began covering this periodical during the year noted in the right column. Most Websites which are listed below have indicated that they will either post, disseminate, compile, archive, cite or alert their own Website users with research-based content from this work. (This list is as current as the copyright date of this publication.)

Abstracting, Website/Indexing Coverage . . . . Year When Coverage Began

- *AGRICOLA Database (AGRICultural OnLine Access): A bibliographic database of citations to the agricultural literature created by the National Agricultural Library and its cooperators* <http://www.natl.usda.gov/ag98> 1989

- *AGRIS* 1989

- *Aluminum Industry Abstracts* <http://www.csa.com> 2003

- *Biosciences Information Service of Biological Abstracts (BIOSIS) a centralized source of life science information* <http://www.biosis.org> 1982

- *BIOSIS Previews: online version of Biological Abstracts and Biological Abstracts/RRM (Reports, Reviews, Meetings); Covers approximately 6,500 life science journals and 2,000 worldwide meetings* 1982

- *Cambridge Scientific Abstracts is a leading publisher of scientific information in print journals, online databases, CD-ROM and via the Internet* <http://www.csa.com> 2003

- *Ceramic Abstracts* <http://www.csa.com> 2003

- *Chemical Abstracts Service–monitors, indexes & abstracts the world's chemical literature, updates this information daily, and makes it accessible through state-of-the-art information services* <http://www.cas.org> 1989

(continued)

(continued)

*Exact start date to come.

(continued)

Special Bibliographic Notes related to special journal issues
(separates) and indexing/abstracting:

- indexing/abstracting services in this list will also cover material in any "separate" that is co-published simultaneously with Haworth's special thematic journal issue or DocuSerial. Indexing/abstracting usually covers material at the article/chapter level.
- monographic co-editions are intended for either non-subscribers or libraries which intend to purchase a second copy for their circulating collections.
- monographic co-editions are reported to all jobbers/wholesalers/approval plans. The source journal is listed as the "series" to assist the prevention of duplicate purchasing in the same manner utilized for books-in-series.
- to facilitate user/access services all indexing/abstracting services are encouraged to utilize the co-indexing entry note indicated at the bottom of the first page of each article/chapter/contribution.
- this is intended to assist a library user of any reference tool (whether print, electronic, online, or CD-ROM) to locate the monographic version if the library has purchased this version but not a subscription to the source journal.
- individual articles/chapters in any Haworth publication are also available through the Haworth Document Delivery Service (HDDS).

Leadership and Management Principles in Libraries in Developing Countries

CONTENTS

ABOUT THE EDITORS

Wei Wei, MA, MLS, is currently Computer Science Librarian at the University of California in Santa Cruz. Prior to her sixteen years at the University of California, she was University Library Associate at the University of Michigan in Ann Arbor from 1986 to 1988. She holds a Master of American Literature degree from the University of Nebraska in Lincoln and a Master of Information and Library Studies degree from the University of Michigan in Ann Arbor.

Wei Wei is active in the Special Libraries Association and the Association's Science and Technology Division and Leadership and Management Division. She is currently Co-Chair of the Association's Diversity Leadership Development Program Committee and Chair of the Leadership and Management Division's International Relations Committee. She was Chair of the Science and Technology Division from 1999 to 2000 and served as chair of its several committees over the past years. She received the 1995 Impossible Award from the Science and Technology Division for her work as Chair of the Division's Public Relations Committee. Wei Wei has given several presentations at the statewide and national level on the survey results of her study on Science and Technology Librarians in California: Their Background, Performance and Expectations. She has authored or co-authored numerous articles such as "Issues Related to the Education and Recruitment of Science/Technology Librarians," "Preparing Academic Research Librarians Today," "Bridge Beyond the Walls: Two Outreach Models at the University of California, Santa Cruz," and a report indexed in the ERIC database on the topic of "Science Library User Survey" at the University of California in Santa Cruz.

Sue O'Neill Johnson, BA, MLS, MPA, is Co-Principal of International Library and Information Associates, Washington, DC. She has a BA in Political Science from Boston University, a Masters in Library and Information Science from the University of Pittsburgh, and a Masters in Public Administration from The American University. She retired from the World Bank as a Senior Information Projects Officer. Ms. Johnson has since been a Consultant to the National Library of Medicine Lister Hill Center, and MEDTAP International. At the Special Libraries Association in 2001, she won the President's Award for creating the Global 2000 Fellowships for librarians in developing countries to attend the Global 2000 Conference in Brighton, England. She was President of the Washington, DC Chapter of SLA in 2001-2002. As President, Ms. Johnson started the Twinning Program for Chapters and Divisions to support memberships for special librarians from developing countries. She was Co-Chair of the International Relations Committee for the Leadership and Management Division in 2002-2003.

Sylvia E. A. Piggott, BA, MLS, currently works as Global Information Solutions Consultant in Montreal, Canada. She received a BA in Cultural Anthropology and an MLS from McGill University, Canada. From 1988 to 2002 she has held a variety of positions at the World Bank and the International Monetary Fund in Washington including Senior Consultant in the Information Solutions Group of the World Bank participating in a variety of activities associated with Evidence-Based Governance in the Electronic Age project, and was awarded a Canadian Trust Fund Grant to take the lead in the Caribbean and Latin American sectors of this project. Ms. Piggott was also Senior Information Solutions Consultant in the World Bank responsible for writing information strategies associated with the Library, Internal Document Unit, and Archives; Deputy Division Chief and Deputy Chief Librarian, Joint World Bank/International Monetary Fund Library and 80 satellite libraries worldwide. She visited and reengineered the World Bank's country office libraries in several African, Southeast Asian, and East Asian countries.

She has fifteen years work experience with the Bank of Montreal, Canada as Senior Manager of Research and Business Information Services and was consultant to major North American companies for several years managing information strategic planning and reengineering of information services.

Ms. Piggott has been an active participant in information science and knowledge sharing professional activities for over 22 years. She was elected President of the Quebec Library Association (Canada) in 1991; President of Eastern Canada Chapter of the Special Libraries Association (SLA) in 1995; selected Information Professional of the Year in 1995 by the Eastern Canada Chapter of SLA; elected President of the International Special Libraries Association (SLA) and Fellow of the Special Libraries Association in 2000; member of the Steering Committee for the Global 2000 international information conference, Brighton, U.K., 1998-2000; elected Chair of the Leadership and Management Division of SLA; and is a frequently invited speaker at international conferences in information management, knowledge management, and information technology topics. She has also written extensively on these subjects.

Introduction

The twenty papers in this volume were selected from those submitted to the Special Libraries Association, Leadership and Management Division's 2003 International Paper Competition for special librarians in developing countries. The winner of the competition was Paiki Muswazi, Swaziland, and Honorable Mentions went to K. A. Raju, India; and to co-authors Muhammad Yaqub Chaudhary and Muhammad Umar Farooq of Kashmir and Islamabad, Pakistan. This volume represents a body of practical experience, problems, lessons and techniques that can be shared and tried by those who want to know more about or deal with the special needs and circumstances of librarians in developing countries.

In the first section, Asia, six papers are from India; and one paper each from China, Indonesia, Pakistan and Sri Lanka. Jagdish Arora discusses the difficulty to motivate and to lead a change of direction to modernize services. Subbiah Arunachalam describes a project of 12 village knowledge centers in a former French territory in southern India. He emphasizes building trust and winning over doubt in entire village populations, using local volunteers, and creating demand for a community kiosk service. Muhammad Yaqub Chaudhary and Muhammad Umar Farook reach beyond the scope of an academic library in Kashmir to gain support from senior management to students through collaboration with the U.S. Information Resource Center in Islamabad using new outreach strategies. P. R. Goswami approaches the problem of maintaining a collection and providing access to the multiple layers of public documents needed for research by using the Delphi technique, and receiving input of experts through structured interviews. V. K. J. Jeevan

---

[Haworth co-indexing entry note]: "Introduction." Wei, Wei, Sue O'Neill Johnson, and Sylvia E. A. Piggott. Co-published simultaneously in *Science & Technology Libraries* (The Haworth Information Press, an imprint of The Haworth Press, Inc.) Vol. 23, No. 2/3, 2002, pp. 1-3; and: *Leadership and Management Principles in Libraries in Developing Countries* (ed: Wei Wei, Sue O'Neill Johnson, and Sylvia E. A. Piggott) The Haworth Information Press, an imprint of The Haworth Press, Inc., 2002, pp. 1-3. Single or multiple copies of this article are available for a fee from The Haworth Document Delivery Service [1-800-HAWORTH, 9:00 a.m. - 5:00 p.m. (EST). E-mail address: docdelivery@haworthpress.com].

Digital Object Identifier: 10.1300/J122v23n02_01

describes modernizing services through a continuum of service improvements and customization.

Following Jeevan in the Asian section, K. A. Raju discusses the effort at the National Institute of Rural Development, Hyderbad, India for "the librarian to change his management style from a mere custodian of information to that of a facilitator, a mentor," since "the environment in which the modern library operates is becoming more and more complex." Wang Fang analyzes the difficulties for the western region of China to develop digital library services, and discusses experiences and lessons learned in solving these problems. Shivanthi Weerasinghe introduces virtual services, thus transforming a corporate library's image from that of a passive unit of lending services to a center of information management and provision. Widharto, in the face of budget declines, sees staff development as the way to provide the services needed by clients, and to attract funding. Key strategies are social networking and marketing, which create the needed continuing education opportunities, and lead to improved services. Finally, the emphasis of Pradnya Yogesh and Alan Dalton's paper is on social networking, and managing an environment for collaboration. One important example is the creation of virtual networking to enable company experts worldwide to share their knowledge.

All of the papers in the second section come from Sub Saharan Africa librarians and deal with a variety of information services. Imo J. Akpan examines the leadership qualities and managerial strategies of an experienced library manager at the Federal Ministry of Industry in Nigeria, emphasizing the necessity for strong leadership in achieving success. Michael Kasusse of Uganda describes the Mobile Patient Library Services, which operates within The Mildmay HIV/AIDS Centre, Kampala, serving patients, care givers, the general public, as well as statutory and voluntary organizations. Foli Kuevidjen's paper looks at the transformation of the American Cultural Center Library in Niamey, Niger, into the Rosa Parks Library, including the interruption of services during and after the first Gulf War.

The paper which was selected as the best in the contest was submitted by Paiki Muswazi, Special Collections Librarian at the University of Swaziland, and is titled "Library and Information Services (LIS) Strategic Planning in a Developing Country: A Case Study." The author describes and critiques the steps followed in the strategic planning process undertaken by the University Library and concludes that the process could be improved in future initiatives of this nature. Josephine Ouedraogo, in her paper "The Application of Leadership and Management Principles and Strategies in an Information Resource Center in

Burkina Faso," states that management principles and leadership strategies applied to an information service works as well as in an enterprise
that makes a profit. In her paper, Mary N. Stevens of Mombassa describes The British Council Management Information Centre and its involvement in The Management Forum, an association of managers in
the region who have come together with the main aim of providing a
channel through which managers across all professions and industries
could share their experience and exchange information in order to promote sustainable development in Africa through better leadership and
governance. The final paper in the second section is by Mariam
Stuurman on "Research Translation in South Africa" which outlines the
activities of the Information Clearinghouse whose role is to create an information system providing for the collection, storage and retrieval of
information with the necessary architecture to support the South African HIV Vaccine Action Campaign.

Two papers in the Eastern Europe section cover very different areas
of information activities. Toshka Borisova's paper provides an overview of the establishment and management of a special journalism library in Bulgaria, which resulted from the unique cooperation between
Freedom Forum Foundation and American University in Bulgaria and
emphasized the implementation of innovations and new technologies.
Muzhgan Nazarova looks in detail at the development of Azerbaijani librarianship over the last 10 years and the changes which have impacted
the development.

Concluding the volume is Grete Pasch's paper from Central America, titled "Cautious but Decisive: Ten Years of Information Services
Implementation at the Universidad Francisco Marroquín in Guatemala." The author gives an overview of the development of this university library and the cautious but decisive strategy employed in the
selection and utilizing of information technology.

It is our hope that our readers will be stimulated by these readings,
and relate to the experiences and lessons presented here from a wide diversity of worldwide locations.

Wei Wei
Sue O'Neill Johnson
Sylvia E. A. Piggott

ASIA

Transforming a Traditional Library
into a Hybrid Library:
Use of Leadership and Managerial Skills
at the Central Library, IIT Delhi

Jagdish Arora

SUMMARY. The article highlights leadership skills and personal traits that were used successfully for transforming a traditional library into a hybrid library in precarious circumstances and conditions that exist in some of the organizations in India. It describes the management techniques, skills and personal traits of a leader that were used to motivate staff members to computerize the library, to improve library services and to transform a traditional library into a hybrid library. *[Article copies available for a fee from The Haworth Document Delivery Service: 1-800-HAWORTH. E-mail address: <docdelivery@haworthpress.com> Website: <http://www.HaworthPress.com> © 2002 by The Haworth Press, Inc. All rights reserved.]*

Jagdish Arora is National Coordinator, INDEST Consortium and Librarian, IIT Bombay (E-mail: j_arora@iitb.ac.in).

[Haworth co-indexing entry note]: "Transforming a Traditional Library into a Hybrid Library: Use of Leadership and Managerial Skills at the Central Library, IIT Delhi." Arora, Jagdish. Co-published simultaneously in *Science & Technology Libraries* (The Haworth Information Press, an imprint of The Haworth Press, Inc.) Vol. 23, No. 2/3, 2002, pp. 5-15; and: *Leadership and Management Principles in Libraries in Developing Countries* (ed: Wei Wei, Sue O'Neill Johnson, and Sylvia E. A. Piggott) The Haworth Information Press, an imprint of The Haworth Press, Inc., 2002, pp. 5-15. Single or multiple copies of this article are available for a fee from The Haworth Document Delivery Service [1-800-HAWORTH, 9:00 a.m. - 5:00 p.m. (EST). E-mail address: docdelivery@haworthpress.com].

http://www.haworthpress.com/web/STL
© 2002 by The Haworth Press, Inc. All rights reserved.
Digital Object Identifier: 10.1300/J122v23n02_02

KEYWORDS. Leadership, motivation, personal traits, library computerization

INTRODUCTION

"May you live in exciting times" says an old Chinese curse. The entire society is under the spell of this curse and libraries are no exception. The libraries, too, are going through a phase of transformation with information technology completely altering their very nature and functions. The library users expect the librarians and library staff to learn new skills and acquire knowledge on systems and services that are prevalent and are being used in modern libraries. The libraries are reinventing themselves in today's networked society to meet these new demands and challenges. While the Chinese curse poses a challenge, it also brings lots of opportunities for the library and information science professionals.

Like any other organization, a library is a collaborative enterprise. Activities and services in a library are the culmination of efforts by various groups and subgroups of people who contributed to the larger goal of reaching users with services rendered to them. Like a chain is as strong as its weakest link, a library is as good as its various components make it. If all its components keep contributing to the larger goal of providing services to the users, the library is successful in achieving its goal; any component that fails to deliver contributes to its overall inefficiency.

The library as an organization requires a leader to lead the team consisting of several groups and subgroups in a cohesive manner with an ultimate aim of rendering services to the users. As the head of the Computer Applications Division at the Central Library, Indian Institute of Technology (IIT) Delhi, I had a unique opportunity to lead a team of people with diverse backgrounds, skills, level of enthusiasm and willingness to work towards computerization of the library.

This article highlights precarious circumstances and working conditions that exist in some of the organizations in India. It describes the management techniques, skills and personal traits of a leader that were used to motivate staff members to computerize the library, to improve the library services and to transform a traditional library into a hybrid library. The article elaborates on steps in transition from traditional to digital library and personal traits that are considered important by the author in leading the team and winning the confidence of authority.

WHERE WE WERE

The task of computerization of the Central Library, Indian Institute of Technology (IIT) Delhi was assigned to me in the year 1998. Although an in-house integrated library software was being developed by a faculty member in the Institute using student manpower without much involvement of library staff, the process had been going on for more than eight years. Only the OPAC was functional, but that too would stop working off and on due to some bugs in the program. Moreover, the bibliographic data available in the Library database was full of errors. Often the bibliographic data in the database did not match the books on the shelves. The Circulation Module and Acquisition Module had gone through a phase of trial, although not very successfully. Since student manpower was employed to work on the package, the process of development was not at all satisfactory. The students would work on the package as a project and leave it for subsequent batches of students to take it up further. Needless to say, this arrangement was not satisfactory. It would take hours to get the catalogue module to work once it was down.

The library has a sub-LAN but it was not functional because the network equipment broke down and no action was taken to restore the library network either by the Librarian or by the then Head of Computer Applications.

WHERE WE ARE

The Library network was restored and augmented as first priority. With purchase of a commercially available library integrated software package called LibSys, all routines in the library are computerized. The data available in the old package was migrated into LibSys after repeated trials. Since the software package developed in-house did not use any standard bibliographic format (i.e., MARC/CCF) for interchange of bibliographic information, it took a few weeks to transfer the data to the commercial software. All books in the Library were barcoded and Library patrons were given barcoded patron cards. In-house facilities were developed for barcoding of books and library patron cards. Students were enrolled as new members as soon as they joined their academic programme. The bibliographic data in the library database has been corrected to a great extent. Moreover, the library has a comprehensive web site that functions as an integrated interface to all computerized services offered by the library. A number of databases developed in-house using CDS/ISIS software package in DOS environment were web-enabled using WWWISIS script. Moreover, impressed with the web-based services of the library, the library was also assigned the task of developing and maintaining the web site for the Institute.

Further, the library has taken several projects from various funding agencies for developing digitised collections in the library. Some of these projects are as follows:

- Developing Digitised Collection in Engineering & Technology (funded by the Ministry of Human Resource Development)
- Internet-based Online Interactive Courseware in Information Technology (Funded by the Ministry of Information Technology)
- Developing Digital Library in Biotechnology (Funded by the Department of Biotechnology)
- Scanning of Documents at the IIT Delhi (Funded by the All India Council of Technical Education)
- Indian Digital Library in Engineering Science and Technology (INDEST) Consortium (Funded by the Ministry of Human Resource Development)

All of the above activities were taken up in a short span of four years, i.e., from 1998 to 2001. A number of projects listed above have been completed successfully.

OUR CIRCUMSTANCES

The qualities, characteristics, and skills deployed to handle a problem are determined by the demands of the circumstances and situation in which we are functioning. "Be a Roman in Rome" it is said. To be effective, one needs to be alert to the reactions of the members of the group, the conditions to which our reactions may lead, and our abilities to handle such reactions. In India we are faced with a peculiar problem, especially in the Government sector or in autonomous bodies with Government funding. The situation that "there is neither a reward for the good work nor is there a punishment for bad work (or no work)." In other words, it does not pay to work hard; there are no direct benefits in terms of promotions or perks. As such the Library did not have a team that was motivated to perform, or had any reason, whatsoever, to be enthusiastic to take up the task of computerization in the library as a challenge. To make things worse, the other senior colleagues in the library were fully convinced that a good performance from a subordinate officer would expose them and put them in a precarious situation. In other words, the team leader for computerization was expected to handle a Herculean task of not only achieving 100% automation of the library but also transforming it into a library with substantial collections in digital media with no support worth its name from other senior colleagues or the top management in the Library with staff that had neither skills nor motivation to work and the Institute authorities, while supportive of providing funds for equipment and software, had their hands tied down with the Government directives to cut down on manpower.

The new responsibility of head of the Computer Applications Division, Central Library at the IIT Delhi, posed challenges that were very unique. The Division was completely paralysed when it was handed over to me. The library LAN was down with network equipment out of service. In any case, there was no service worth its name that was made available to users on the network. Moreover, there were a lot of expectations from the authorities and users community since I had just returned from a sabbatical as a Fulbright Fellow in Library and Information Science. I already enjoyed a good reputation in the eyes of authorities and users for the good job I had done in the Serials Division before going on the sabbatical leave for the Fulbright Fellowship in the Library and Information Science in 1997-98. While my contributions and services at the Serials Division was duly acknowledged by the library users and the faculty, the change in responsibility gave me an opportunity to implement new skills acquired by me during my Fulbright sojourn. The Institute authority and the users expected new changes and developments, having faith in my capabilities and devotion to work. The reputation that I had built in the eyes of authorities gave me support in terms of additional fundings, manpower, moral support, etc., that would not have been forthcoming if not for the reputation I had earned.

I was fully aware that I had an uphill task that required a lot of patience, hard-work, belief in oneself, and traits that my team members could look up to and follow. Leadership is all about taking up responsibilities, facilitating, directing, guiding, steering, acting as a conduit and inspiring and motivating the members of your team. The leader requires a few basic personal traits and a range of techniques for implementing his or her goals and vision.

PERSONAL TRAITS

Positive Attitude

The most important trait a leader should have is a positive attitude. Always ask yourself "how can it be done." Never start with "why it cannot be done." Most people adopt the strategy of "excuse management," they go to a great length finding excuses as to why a job cannot be done rather than exploring the possibilities of how it can be done.

Lead by Example

The leader of a team needs to lead by example. You cannot expect your team to follow you unless you literally lead them in all spheres of activities, be it in work, punctuality, sincerity or the number of hours that you put in on the job. You need to be the first to reach the workplace, if you expect your teammates to be punctual. You cannot expect people to be punctual unless you yourself are punctual. Moreover, you are also required to lead your team in technological skills. You need to update yourself with new skills so that you can talk to your IT personnel in their own lingua-franca. Your teammates should be fully convinced that you are one step ahead of them to get their respect.

Love Your Job, Have a Passion for It and Take It Personally

In order to be successful, it is important to love your job and demonstrate passion for it. Several colleagues advised me not to take things personally, if someone gets in the way of accomplishing your assigned job, deal with it as if you would deal with any other official matter. However, if you have passion for your work, you need to take things personally and deal with them passionately. While constructive criticism aimed at improving functions and services should be welcomed, actions that are designed and planted to create hurdles need to be dealt with firm hands. While being flexible if the circumstances demand is also necessary, it is also important to be firm, if the situation so demands. Without mixing words, it should be made clear to one and all that the stumbling blocks planted intentionally in the path of progress will not be tolerated.

Character in Leadership

Character for a leader stands for self-discipline, loyalty, readiness to accept responsibility and willingness to accept mistakes. The character of a leader should also have quality of modesty, selflessness, willingness to sacrifice, humility and faith in oneself and fellow team members.

Be Sincere

The team leader needs to be sincere to his/her work; that needs to be reflected in words, deeds and actions. Your superiors, your peers and subordinate staff should be able to see your sincerity to the core. The people looking for a role model should see it in you. Your superiors should be able to see themselves in you. More than everything else you should believe in yourself sincerely and it can not be superficial or faked. Moreover, do not expect everyone to respect your sincerity.

IMPLEMENTATIONS OF TECHNIQUES: HOW TO LEAD

Vision

As a leader, it is important that you have a well-defined vision and goal that are clear to your team. A leader should be able to plan and aim not only for the immediate present but also beyond it. As a leader, you should be able to communicate with your team members as well as with the authorities convincingly and with conviction. Moreover, you need to plan thoroughly before putting things into action. Planning may be done involving your superiors, your staff members or alone, depending upon the circumstances.

Facilitate and Be Flexible

Once your vision and goals are defined, as a team leader it is your responsibility to facilitate all requirements of your team members, be it physical infrastructure, computing infrastructure, manpower or any other. The facilitation also includes mentoring and imparting training to the members of the team. The process of facilitation also involves recognizing strengths and weaknesses of members of your team and using them to the maximum for the advantage of your organization. With the purchase of a commercial package at the library, several training programmes were organized on LibSys software package at various levels. All staff members of the library were trained in the use of LibSys. Training was offered at a basic level as well as at advanced levels. Training programmes were also organized on web site design as well as on digital libraries. People from other institutions were also invited to participate in IIT training sessions. The process of facilitation, therefore, did not reach to the team alone but was also extended to other professional colleagues.

Being flexible is also an important strategy to achieve your goals and vision. With your goals and vision well defined, being flexible about how to get there could be the key to success. Flexibility allows you to respond to a situation depending upon the expected reactions and your ability to handle them.

Motivate

The three most important motivating factors for an employee are: (i) reward for performance; (ii) punishment for non-performance; and (iii) technology as a motivating factor. In an environment where you do not have liberty to either reward for good performance or punish for non-performance, a leader's options are restricted to rewarding good performance with small gestures like sponsoring your employees to conferences and workshops, getting them honoraria from your project funds and involving them in tasks that they consider important.

The technology itself serves as a motivating factor for people who have a zeal to learn. Several people from different sections in my library approached me to learn about computers although their assigned job did not involve using computers. They came to learn on their own time; they learned the basics of using computers and the library software package used by the library and started attending to jobs that were not their assigned jobs. One thing triggered another. It snowballed into a movement where most of the library manpower was computer literate. The library attendants on the circulation counter learned to use computers for issuing books, the library attendants with duties to shelve the books started using the catalogue search and OPAC modules to help users to locate the books. They started using computers to generate labels for barcoding the books. Technology indeed proved to be a motivating factor in an otherwise closed atmosphere.

Nurture Your Followers

It is important that we recognize talent amongst our colleagues and motivate them. People with talents, potentials and zeal to learn need to be recognized and encouraged. They may be coached separately to learn new skills in information technology. People completely unconnected with computerization activity may be used to do jobs that had nothing to do with their routine assignments and they would happily do it in their spare time just because technology attracted them and it gave them immense satisfaction to do things using computers. Getting a printout for jobs done by them was very exciting and fulfilling for them.

Command Respect, Do Not Demand It

People respect you for your work. Never expect people to respect you for your position. No one respects you for your age or position. Respect is mutual, you must respect others before they can reciprocate.

Let Your Actions Speak for Themselves

Do not brag about your plans or what you are set to achieve, work methodically and with zeal in your assigned work and projects and let the deliverable speak for themselves.

Recognize the Opportunity, Grab It As It Comes and Take Responsibilities

We are passing through a revolution that has unsettled its player. There are several new information technologies that are new to every one. Enterprising individuals with the right skills can put them to innovative use in library and information science. The recent developments in information technology offer several opportunities that one must grab in spite of limitations in terms of time, manpower, skills and a "No rewards" policy. At my Institute, looking at the library web site created by the Computer Applications Division in the library, the library was offered the job of redoing the web site of the Institute. We took this responsibility without a hitch in spite of severe limitations that we had in terms of manpower, skills required, raised hopes, and criticism from peers, with a hope that such an opportunity would put us on a pedestal where the visibility of the library within the organization would be at its peak. A leader of the team would consider it important to take up responsibilities assessing the given situation that offer us an opportunity to enhance the reputation of the library in the Institute.

The library not only did a good job on the Institute web site but also gained new skills, heightened reputation, equipment and manpower. What started as a one-year experimental project was given to the library as a permanent assignment, with manpower, money and other perks.

The library also rose to other occasions when required. For example, we were asked to make a CD consisting of selected publications of the Institute to be given to dignitaries visiting the Institute. Once again we geared up to put our act together and gained the skills required to produce a CD with integrated multimedia. The final product was delightfully well received. Once again, the library established its place in the Institute as a technologically advanced enterprise.

Taking responsibility also means that we accept our successes as well as our failures. Do not blame others for your failures. However, learn from your mistake and your experiences. For example, we decided to outsource the job of getting the barcoded patron cards produced from the external outfit. Soon we found that the job was taking much more time and patron cards produced by the external outfit had several mistakes that had to be corrected, consuming more time. The library users had to wait for months to get their barcoded patron cards. We realized our mistake and took the decision to produce patron cards in-house. The facilities for producing bar-coded patron cards was, therefore, established in-house.

Write Projects

The changing scenario offers a lot of challenges and opportunities. If you keep abreast with the changing technologies, it should be possible for you to recognize new projects and avenues. Taking up new projects that are not a part of your assigned jobs would give you an insight into various aspects of technology and its applications. The sponsored projects bring funds, allow you to recruit fresh manpower on contract, provide you an opportunity to delve deep into the new technology and its applications. Moreover, project funds provide flexibilities that are not available to you from the funds available through normal Institute grants. At IIT Delhi we made it a point to apply for new projects every year.

Project funds, however, come with strings attached. The fund providers expect regular updates, timely reports, workshops and demonstrations of products and services developed under the project. It is important that formalities spelled out by the fund providers are duly fulfilled. The fund providers also require justification for their investments. Part of the project leader's job is to help them justify that their judgment to fund you was not wrong. Time management is one of the very important aspects of project management. You should be ready with deliverables within the given time frame. The funds allotted should be spent in the given time period with deliverables to the satisfaction of fund providers.

CONCLUSION

While it is important to have traits of a leader, it is more important to have determination, complete devotion and sincerity that ultimately help you to achieve your defined goals. We in India believe in the theory of "Karma" that says we should completely devote ourselves to our assigned work irrespective of the fact whether you get results or you don't.

The Fulbright Fellowship helped me to learn new skills, especially web designing, computer graphics and multimedia applications and scanning technologies. It would not have been possible for me to learn all these new skills, if it was not for the Fulbright Fellowship that gave me an opportunity to learn more skills, to meet with the stalwarts in the field and to visit important libraries and projects in action. The Fellowship also gave me an opportunity to observe functioning of American organizations and compare them with the governing system in India.

The Role of Leadership
and Innovative Management
in Building Rural Knowledge Centers
to Reach the "Unreached"

Subbiah Arunachalam

SUMMARY. This paper describes the village knowledge centers in Pondicherry, southern India, which aim to empower the poor and the marginalized through information technology-enabled information access. Mobilizing people and understanding their context and needs on the one hand and marshaling the content that is relevant to the people's needs and choosing the appropriate mix of technologies to reach the information to the people when they need it on the other pose considerable challenges. How these challenges were faced by the development agency which initiated the programme is analyzed with a view to highlighting the role played by quality leadership and innovative management. *[Article copies available for a fee from The Haworth Document Delivery Service: 1-800-HAWORTH. E-mail address: <docdelivery@haworthpress.com> Website: <http://www.HaworthPress.com> © 2002 by The Haworth Press, Inc. All rights reserved.]*

Subbiah Arunachalam, MS, is a Distinguished Fellow in Information Science at M S Swaminathan Research Foundation, India.

Address correspondence to: Subbiah Arunachalam, M S Swaminathan Research Foundation, Third Cross Street, Taramani Institutional Area, Chennai 600 113, India (E-mail: arun@mssrf.res.in).

The project described in this paper is funded by the International Development Research Center (IDRC), Ottawa, and the Canadian International Development Agency.

[Haworth co-indexing entry note]: "The Role of Leadership and Innovative Management in Building Rural Knowledge Centers to Reach the 'Unreached.' " Arunachalam, Subbiah. Co-published simultaneously in *Science & Technology Libraries* (The Haworth Information Press, an imprint of The Haworth Press, Inc.) Vol. 23, No. 2/3, 2002, pp. 17-24; and: *Leadership and Management Principles in Libraries in Developing Countries* (ed: Wei Wei, Sue O'Neill Johnson, and Sylvia E. A. Piggott) The Haworth Information Press, an imprint of The Haworth Press, Inc., 2002, pp. 17-24. Single or multiple copies of this article are available for a fee from The Haworth Document Delivery Service [1-800-HAWORTH, 9:00 a.m. - 5:00 p.m. (EST). E-mail address: docdelivery@haworthpress.com].

Digital Object Identifier: 10.1300/J122v23n02_03

KEYWORDS. Rural knowledge center, information access, community ownership

The words 'libraries' and 'information centers' evoke in our minds images of special libraries, academic libraries, public libraries and children's libraries in affluent towns and cities. All of these put together, including the Internet, the Open Archives and the emerging digital libraries, serve only a small fraction of humankind. A vast majority of people continue to live with virtually no access to knowledge that they can use in their daily lives. Despite all the talk about alleviating poverty and ushering in development, the numbers of such people are increasing. The world is a terribly unequal place. As someone pointed out, the inequality is so disturbing that wealthy nations pursue drugs to treat baldness, erectile dysfunction and obesity, and depression in dogs, while elsewhere millions are so poor that they suffer from endemic hunger and are sick or dying from preventable or treatable infectious and parasitic diseases. The poor of the world need and can benefit from information and knowledge, but in their struggle to keep body and soul together they cannot think of information and libraries. The M S Swaminathan Research Foundation (MSSRF), a non-Governmental organization located in Chennai, India, wanted to change all that in one small corner of the world.

The Foundation set up a project in southern India, with funding from the International Development Research Center, Ottawa, Canada, for reaching the most urgently needed information to the hitherto unreached. Based on Mahatma Gandhi's philosophy of *Antyodaya* (similar to Ruskin's philosophy of 'unto the last'), the project team works with the people very closely and tries to meet the information needs of the poorest and the marginalized. The goals of the project are determined by the people, their context and their needs and wants rather than by the technologies that are available. The project involves both social mobilization and deployment of technologies, and it is important to optimize both the resources available and the effort in order to maximize benefits to the users of the services. This paper aims to bring out the leadership and innovative management practices that have led to the success of the project.

EMPOWERING THE POOR THROUGH IT-ENABLED INFORMATION ACCESS

While scholars, scientists and librarians were worrying about the 'serials crisis,' debating how to wrest control of communication channels such as journals from the clutches of greedy commercial publishers, and setting up a 'Public Library of Science' and e-print archives, MSSRF was looking at empowering the poor and the downtrodden in rural India and making a difference in their lives through better access to knowledge. Inspired by a visionary leader, M S Swaminathan, one of the twenty most influential Asians of the 20th century according to *Time* magazine, the team of not-so-highly qualified young people has built 'knowledge centers' in 12 villages in the former French territory of Pondicherry, about 150 km south of Madras. The Foundation, established in 1988, works in the areas of sustainable development, eco-technology, improving livelihood opportunities of the rural poor and women in particular, biodiversity, and food and nutrition security. It is both a think tank and a grassroots organization.

Taking knowledge to rural areas is nothing new in southern India. It was there, in the medium-sized town of Mannargudi in Tamil Nadu, that the late Prof. S R Ranganathan started the movement of mobile libraries on 21 October 1931 when he took books and magazines on a bullock cart to reach his rural clients. The modern day followers of Ranganathan, working at the M S Swaminathan Research Foundation, are not using a bullock cart. They are not even using a car or a motorbike. They have moved with the times and are using modern information and communication technologies (ICTs) to gather and disseminate information, without baffling the villagers with technology.

The 12 village knowledge centers are connected by a hybrid wired and wireless network–consisting of personal computers, telephones and modems, VHF duplex radio devices, spread spectrum and email and Internet connectivity through dial up telephone lines and VSAT–that facilitates both voice and data transfer. Wireless links are used to connect villages without electricity. Solar energy is used to run the computers in the knowledge centers so services could continue uninterrupted even during power failures, which are frequent in these villages. The centers provide the villagers with the information they want and need and can use readily to improve their lives. This includes information on crops, farm practices, animal husbandry, health, education, government entitlements, bus timings, weather, fishing, employment opportunities, micro-enterprises, yellow pages, etc. The knowledge centers are open to all, irrespective of age, sex, religion, caste, and level of literacy and education. The entire project reflects the holistic philosophy of Swaminathan, which emphasizes an integrated pro-poor, pro-women and pro-Nature approach to development. Because it would be impossible to provide the same level of access to ICT tools to all the people in the world as is currently the norm in the affluent countries, the MSSRF team thought of a more practical model: community ownership of technological tools, community-based access and resource sharing to tackle the problem of serving a huge population with limited resources. All knowledge centers use the local language, i.e., Tamil, and multimedia (to facilitate use by illiterate users) and encourage collective action. Technologies are not used simply because they are there; they are used only when there are specific needs that they can address. The knowledge centers also use blackboards, billboards, public address systems and a twice-monthly community newspaper to reach out to a broad spectrum of people. One of the strengths of the MSSRF team is its admirable ability to blend traditional and modern technologies. Horses for courses, as they say.

A project of this kind cannot succeed unless the community has a sense of ownership and participation right from the beginning. Knowledge centers are set up only when the local people express a need for them. The community provides quality space and electricity and nominates volunteers. MSSRF provide the technology, training and managerial help. This bottom-up exercise began with local volunteers polling the community to find out what they want and what they already have. The initial survey of several thousand households in the region revealed that there were very few public access telephones (often non-operational), reading rooms or libraries and post offices. But there were a large number of television sets and the village families were eagerly watching Tamil movies shown on television all days of the week. That was proof enough that the villagers were ready to invest in something if they found some value in it. They would welcome the knowledge centers if they provided information that is perceived to be of value by the local community. MSSRF trained local volunteers to collect information from different sources, such as the nearby meteorological office, markets, government departments, primary health centers, educational institutions, and traders selling seeds, fertilizers, and pesticides. The information is fed into an intranet-type network, and access to the information is provided through nodes in different villages. There are now about 100 databases, which are updated frequently. Each center is manned by at least two volunteers at any given time.

About 300 users walk into these centers on an average day. They get answers to their queries, use computers (for typing documents, filling in forms, playing games, learning from CD-ROM educational material, etc.), read newspapers, and make telephone calls. The work of the centers is monitored through monthly participatory appraisal meetings in which MSSRF staff, knowledge center volunteers and community representatives take part. All centers maintain user registers. As mere information or knowledge cannot lead to development, the centers provide assistance to the community in seeking employment, setting up self-help groups and microenterprises, and getting micro-credit. Thus it is a holistic (or integrated) program.

The centers have been running for more than five years, and new centers are being opened as and when there is a demand and new databases are added and the range of services is extended.

RECOGNITION

The knowledge centers have gained some recognition for ingenuity and creativity in the use of technology. For example, the project won the Motorola Dispatch Solution Gold Award[1] for 1999 "for supply of useful information in order to improve quality of life," and the Stockholm Challenge Award for 2001 in the category 'A Global Village' for "contribution in the global movement of building a better Information Society for all." To quote the Stockholm Jury: "This project is a wonderful example of the benefits of IT, and of the power of information and opportunity."[2]

After visiting the knowledge centers, Prof. Bruce Alberts, President of the U.S. National Academy of Sciences, made these comments: "As scientists we need to learn from these experiments, so as to make a science out of connecting the world to knowledge resources. With the technology moving so fast, it is critical to learn by doing it this way, so that we learn how to make the next wave of technology even more useful for productive and suitable economic development."[3] In our knowledge centers Alberts sees the seeds of a virtual university: "I envision a global electronic network that connects scientists to people at all levels–farmers' organizations and village women, for example. The network will allow them to easily access the scientific and technical knowledge that they need to solve problems and enhance the quality of their lives, as well as to communicate their own insights and needs back to scientists."[4] He is "enormously impressed with the quality of thought that has gone into this project, as well as by the energy, dedication, and skill of the young Indian scientists who are carrying it out."[4]

Alfonso Gumucio Dagron, the well-known development communication expert, is very appreciative of the development of local databases and local web pages relevant to the local community and says "this is why the village knowledge centers in Pondicherry are such an important and coherent experience."[5] For him, this project provides a paradigm for the future direction of development.

LEADERSHIP AND MANAGEMENT PRINCIPLES APPLIED

First, the grand vision of using ICTs for rural development through enhanced access to information. Swaminathan asked "If ICTs can benefit the advanced countries and the rich everywhere, why can't we press them into service to help the poor?" He did it at a time when there was considerable skepticism among donor agencies on investing in ICTs as against investing in aid for food, healthcare, education, etc. The MSSRF team thought it could use ICTs as a crosscutting theme that can benefit other sectors like agriculture, health and education and the results proved it right.

Second, the project was participatory right from Day One. The relation between MSSRF and the village community is one of partnership in progress, and not donor and recipient. The entire village community–men and women, landed gentry and the landless, educated and the illiterate–was consulted and involved. The MSSRF team adopted a policy of 'inclusiveness.' Appreciating this aspect of the program, Bruce Alberts says: "My experience in India has made it clear to me that our nation would be much more successful in such endeavors if we were humble enough to incorporate the potential beneficiaries of a service into its initial planning."[4] The village volunteers do much of the work, and many of them are women, thus giving them status and influence in their communities.

Third, the project called for considerable managerial skills. On the one hand the MSSRF scientists had to mobilize the entire people of the many villages they work in and get accepted by them. That was quite a task. They needed to liaise with government officials, local institutions, traders, and a number of others. They needed to form self-help groups, help in setting up micro-enterprises, arrange micro-credit, and help market the products coming out of micro-enterprises. Above all, they must work out a smooth withdrawal strategy, ensuring that the knowledge centers, self-help groups, micro-enterprises, etc., will continue to function and with greater efficiency, even after they withdraw.

Fourth, the knowledge centers were handling a mix of technologies and the mix had to be smart enough to meet the project's objectives. They also needed to train the local volunteers in their use (see Figure 1). Thus there was the twin challenge of managing social mobilization on the one hand and technology management on the other, and bringing these two together to reap maximum synergy. The project team has an open mind on technology. In the beginning it started with somewhat high-end technologies such as interconnected computers and communication technologies, but the team found even traditional technologies had an important role to play. The community newspaper is read avidly by many. About 7,500 copies of this newspaper are distributed free in about 30 villages. The centers use blackboards and billboards to display the latest news and announcements. Wave height information for the Pondicherry coast is downloaded every day from a U.S. Navy Web site and transmitted to the knowledge centers in coastal villages, where the volunteers use the age-old public address system to broadcast the audio file. It is clear that simply because something is old it need not be discarded.

Fifth, widespread access to information can lead to changes in social equations. For example, many villagers are now aware of government entitlements and they go and ask for them. The officials are now receiving more inquiries and more claims than ever before. In another example, landlords who pay part of the wages to their landless laborers in kind can no longer give lower quantities of whatever they are giving in kind, as the prices are known to everybody. The officials who are bombarded with queries and the landlords may not like what is happening. There have, in fact, been occasions when certain landlords have brought in labor from outside the village when the local labor demanded the right quantity of rice given as wages in kind. Such situations require considerable tact and persuasive skills to sort out. Right now, the project leader is tackling such issues.

In the early phase of the project, three knowledge centers set up at private residences had to be closed, as the services did not reach all sections of the people in the village and were monopolized by the relatives and friends of the residents.

When the project became well known and started receiving considerable media attention and accolades from eminent people around the world, the MSSRF staff, the volunteers and the villagers were all happy, but they did not allow any of this to make them complacent. All of them continue to work hard to achieve their goal of helping the poor in these villages get out of the poverty trap, the raison d'etre for everything the Foundation does.

On the whole, these knowledge centers posed many challenges to the organization's skills in leadership and management, and by and large the MSSRF team seems to have overcome these challenges.

FIGURE 1. Knowledge Centers Are Always Busy

Used with permission.

REFERENCES

1. Motorola, DSA 1999 Dispatch Solution Award Announcement.

2. Stockholm Challenge Award Jury's Motivations on the Winning Projects, Category Global Village 2001, <http://www.challenge.stockholm.se/new_tavlande_index.html>.

3. Alberts, B. Science for African Development, Talk delivered at the Substantive Session of the Economic and Social Council of the United Nations, *Geneva, Switzerland, July 17, 2001.*

4. Alberts, B. Science and the World's Future, President's Address, 136th Annual Meeting, Washington, DC, April 26, 1999.

5. Alfonso Gumucio Dagron, contribution to the Making Waves discussion forum, dated 20 June 2001.

The Application of Leadership and Management Principles in Libraries: A Case Study of the Central Library and Kashmir Information Resource Center (KIRC), The University of Azad Jammu and Kashmir

Muhammad Yaqub Chaudhary
Muhammad Umar Farooq

SUMMARY. This essay elaborates on how a librarian of the developing country used some of the principles for the progress of his library. The librarians of the developing countries work under circumstances that might be unusual for the developed world. Here, a library leader has to apply diverse skills, strategies and principles for the advancement of his/her library. Although many of them are common, however, some of the leadership principles and management strategies may vary with the na-

Muhammad Yaqub Chaudhary is Chief Librarian, The University of Azad Jammu and Kashmir, Muzzaffarabad, Azad Kashmir.

Muhammad Umar Farooq is Reference Specialist, Information Resource Center (IRC), U.S. Embassy Islamabad, Pakistan.

[Haworth co-indexing entry note]: "The Application of Leadership and Management Principles in Libraries: A Case Study of the Central Library and Kashmir Information Resource Center (KIRC), The University of Azad Jammu and Kashmir." Chaudhary, Muhammad Yaqub, and Muhammad Umar Farooq. Co-published simultaneously in *Science & Technology Libraries* (The Haworth Information Press, an imprint of The Haworth Press, Inc.) Vol. 23, No. 2/3, 2002, pp. 25-33; and: *Leadership and Management Principles in Libraries in Developing Countries* (ed: Wei Wei, Sue O'Neill Johnson, and Sylvia E. A. Piggott) The Haworth Information Press, an imprint of The Haworth Press, Inc., 2002, pp. 25-33. Single or multiple copies of this article are available for a fee from The Haworth Document Delivery Service [1-800-HAWORTH, 9:00 a.m. - 5:00 p.m. (EST). E-mail address: docdelivery@haworthpress.com].

Digital Object Identifier: 10.1300/J122v23n02_04

ture, scope, size, and strategic position of a library. More importantly, the management strategy of a librarian depends upon the psychology, nature and behavior of a community in which he/she serves. Professional as well as personal competencies are not developed overnight. A true librarian learns lessons from the past and then plans for the future. *[Article copies available for a fee from The Haworth Document Delivery Service: 1-800-HAWORTH. E-mail address: <docdelivery@haworthpress.com> Website: <http://www.HaworthPress.com> © 2002 by The Haworth Press, Inc. All rights reserved.]*

KEYWORDS. Academic librarians as information leaders, administration–university libraries–developing countries, community–university libraries–developing countries, competencies for academic librarians, Information Partnership Program, Kashmir Information Resource Center (KIRC), leadership principles–academic librarians, management skills–academic librarians, University of Azad Jammu and Kashmir, university libraries of developing countries

INTRODUCTION AND BACKGROUND

The University of Azad Jammu and Kashmir is a public university and offers mostly science and technology programs. The University was established in 1980 with limited resources. The federal government of Pakistan and the government of Azad Jammu and Kashmir are the primary funding bodies of the University. Even though the university is situated in a politically disturbed and economically backward remote area, it flourished rapidly, overcoming many hurdles along the way.

Like the University in general, the Library and Information Resource Center had several hurdles of its own to overcome as well. I joined the University fifteen years ago. At that time the library consisted of one room and the books were kept in locked shelves. The budget for the library was so meager that one could only buy some daily newspapers. In general, there was very little attraction for readers, and less for faculty and students. There were some books but they were out-dated and irrelevant to the teaching programs. Most budget requests went unheeded.

In addition to these economic hurdles, there was campus unrest among students and faculty. Strikes were observed regularly by both students and university employees. The library was not spared from this campus unrest: at one point a protesting group sealed the doors of the

University offices and library with elfi, which is a type of sticky gum. The library was able to weather the storm without further harm because I was able to convince the leaders of the strike not to disturb the library. Instead, I explained that they could utilize the library for their meetings and read newspapers during their strike hours.

As if these economic and political hurdles were not enough, the University and library had to overcome geography: The University is spread across an area of over 5,000 square miles, covering the entire State of Azad Jammu and Kashmir. The State of Azad Jammu and Kashmir includes five districts, and the University was planned as a multi-campus institution spreading across all districts. These districts are not connected directly by roads because of difficult and inaccessible high mountains. In fact, one has to travel through Pakistan to reach some of the more distant areas.

This unique combination of politics, economics and geography makes the task of a Chief Librarian more challenging and complicated. As Chief Librarian I had to adopt various leadership and management principles and strategies to cope with the situation. Some of these techniques may not fall in the standard list of SLA's "*Competencies for Special Librarians of the 21st Century,*" or in ARL/OCLC's "*The Keystone Principles for Academic Libraries,*" or even in the Librarians of the 21st Century's "*Leadership and Management Principles in Libraries.*" But my strategies worked well enough and hopefully will prove to be a great success story of a Library and Information Resource Center of a developing country.

KEY LEADERSHIP AND MANAGEMENT PRINCIPLES

Keeping in mind the above mentioned challenges, I set my own strategy as follows:

1. If There's a Will, There's a Way
2. First Deserve, then Desire
3. Exposure to Higher Authority
4. Exposure to Others
5. Service Without Asking
6. Look for Alternative Resources
7. Self Education and Improvements
8. Public Relations with Seniors, Juniors and Readers
9. Retreat but Never Surrender
10. Acknowledgements and Thanks

This essay elaborates on how I used some of the above mentioned principles in the development of the library. If There's a Will, There's a Way. Although cliched, no plan of action can begin without a desire to achieve a particular goal. Any effort requires self-confidence, commitment and dedication. I knew what I wanted to achieve, I had confidence in my ability to get it, and I was willing to commit to the time and effort required to achieve my goal.

FIRST DESERVE, THEN DESIRE

I strongly believe in the principle, "First Deserve, then Desire." I applied this principle in the area of service to the community: In order to get the things I desired for the library to improve service to the community, I first had to demonstrate that I deserved them. For example, the library used to open only for 6 hours a day. I managed to keep the library open for 12 hours a day without demanding extra staff and facilities. In addition, a TV, VCR and cable connection are now available in the library to attract those people who come to the library for these alternate forms of information and entertainment. Just two years ago, there was no Internet Service Provider in this region. At that time, I signed an Information Partnership Program with the American Information Resource Center, U.S. Embassy Islamabad. This allowed the library to get information by telephone, fax and postal service. The Information Partnership Program ensured timely and high quality reference and research services for the targeted audiences of my library. Having accomplished so much on my own, it is easier to justify future requests for help and support: I am able to show that I deserve what I ask for because I improved community service a great deal already.

EXPOSURE TO HIGHER AUTHORITY

One of the techniques I used may be called "Exposure to the Boss." For example, four years ago the current Vice Chancellor of the University was appointed. Although he was a retired civil servant he seemed to be a friend of the library. In order to increase his awareness of the library, i.e., "exposure to the boss," I arranged a meeting between him and the Information Resource Officer (IRO) and the other staff of the state of the art Information Resource Center (IRC) of the U.S. Embassy Islamabad. Arranging this meeting served two purposes. First, the Vice Chancellor was able to see first hand the resources, people and services available at such a unique library as the IRC. Second, and more importantly, by meeting with the Vice Chancellor and arranging the meeting between him and the IRC I got the chance to express my desire to transform my traditional library into a model resource center like the IRC. The Vice Chancellor principally agreed. Even though he was not able to provide much fiscal support due to the scarcity of funds, I requested and was provided with much moral support in my continuing efforts to create resources myself from national and international donor agencies. Because of solicited donations of books, journals, audiovisual materials, and computers from the U.S. Embassy, British Council, Asia Foundation and Netherlands Library Development Program, the library has shaped up to be a modern library of which the University can be proud. This is an example of how "exposure to the boss" is an important element of library management; it is too easy for University administration to lose sight of the library, especially on such a vast campus.

EXPOSURE TO OTHERS

When an Internet facility was launched in Kashmir I arranged a daylong workshop at the IRC for a group of students, faculty members, and the administrative staff, including the Vice Chancellor of the University. According to the IRC staff, it was the highest level academic workshop they had ever arranged. I arranged many seminars and events in the library Conference Hall to attract University staff and other people from the community. Even the President and Prime Minister of the State participated in these events, and the University library got good media coverage because of the presence of these VIPs. Another example of exposure to others is when I approached Pakistan Television (PTV) to hold a program on librarianship. I conducted and coordinated a one-hour program on "Career Choice in Library and Information Science," in which representatives from teaching departments, central libraries and students from all over the country participated. This program was telecast many times on all the channels of PTV. This kind of exposure is invaluable to the success of a University library, especially one facing the various hurdles described at the beginning of this article.

SERVICE WITHOUT ASKING

By going beyond the scope of an academic library, I opened the resources of the University library to the President, Prime Minister, Judiciary, and Bureaucracy by including their names on the mailing list. This initiative produced positive results; once the President called me personally and asked for the background and current materials on "Kashmir Conflict" for his lecture at the National Defense College, Rawalpindi. This kind of service without asking goes a long way to establishing the prestige and profile of the library.

LOOK FOR ALTERNATIVE RESOURCES

As mentioned before, due to limited resources the library was unable to subscribe to any academic databases; however, under the Information Partnership Program, the library has been using the online resources of the IRC. Despite this resource, I wished to have direct access to some academic databases in order to let the faculty in the University research the literature of their disciplines. I kept looking for alternative sources to get funding for the online databases. Recently I approached the Pakistan Scientific and Technological Information Center (PASTIC) and succeeded in getting one million rupees for a subscription to OCLC, NEXIS, ProQuest, and EbscoHost. Before that, I already had a signed pact with COMSTECH database network. I preferred a scheme for the establishment of a Kashmir Information Resource Center (KIRC) similar to the IRC. The University syndicate has approved it because most of the faculty and administration were convinced; these same faculty and administration had already visited the IRC, as discussed above. This is a good example of how practicing these 10 principles together support each other; exposure to others made my search for alternative resources successful.

SELF-EDUCATION AND IMPROVEMENTS

I received my master's degree in 1971 and therefore I was behind the latest developments in our profession. I struggled hard to keep myself abreast of new information by attending seminars/workshops/short courses and by reading professional literature. Since 2000 I have attended such activities in the United States and in Europe as well. I am a life member of the Pakistan Library Association, Punjab Library Association, Sir Syed Memorial Society, Sustainable Development Policy Institute, SLA, ALA, CLA, IFLA, CILIP . . . This continuing self-education and professional improvement has given me professional confidence, a necessary principle as discussed above.

PUBLIC RELATIONS WITH SENIORS, JUNIORS AND READERS

In my view, a librarian should be social and proactive. He should have strong ties with his supervisor, colleagues and his subordinates. This year, I arranged a get together to celebrate the Eid Festival (an annual Muslim festival like Christmas) in the library. The faculty, administrative staff and their kids participated in the event. This was a social and religious gathering in an academic environment. We displayed the information about "Eid" in electronic and print form and served tea and sweets to guests. The Vice Chancellor was very pleased with efforts and the work of the library; on request he wrote and delivered a letter of appreciation and a cash reward to my staff in a public ceremony. I am always in search of opportunities to give some kind of formal or informal service to my seniors. It is our routine to put information relating to scholarships, jobs, and social activities on the library's notice board. Most of the students ask for our guidance regarding admissions abroad.

THANKS AND ACKNOWLEDGEMENTS

Since there was no financial resources for purchasing the books and library materials that we wanted, I decided to approach the different donor agencies in Pakistan such as the IRC, Asia Foundation, British Council. This effort succeeded in getting new materials as well as their weeded out books and journals. Whenever I get a donation I send a letter of thanks to the donor agency. I persuaded my Vice Chancellor to send a note of thanks with the request for more reading materials. Within a few years, the library acquired so much material that the shelves were not sufficient and I persuaded the Finance Department to purchase more shelves. A time came when there was no space even for more shelves. I then requested the Vice Chancellor to make arrangements for a new building and, after a long struggle, the library was shifted to the most beautiful and functional building of the University, which was actually built for the Institute of Kashmir Studies. I kept up my struggle for a new building for the library; luckily, the government awarded a huge grant for this purpose and now this building is under construction.

It is interesting that about two hundred serials are received in the library solely based on requests and solicitations and prompt and regular letters of acknowledgement and thanks without spending a penny.

LESSONS LEARNED

Below are some lessons I learned in my professional career:

1. There is no ideal situation for a librarian. He has to find out his own ways to serve the community. The limited financial resources are the common hurdles for the librarians of the developing countries. Therefore, a librarian of the developing country has to be proactive for finding the funding and donations for the development of his library.
2. Continuing education and professional training courses are essential for librarians. The traditional and formal professional degree is not sufficient for a librarian to meet the challenges of the information age.
3. Sometimes a librarian finds one method useless or not sufficient to achieve the desired goals and objectives. Therefore, he has to change the way and test another method. Similarly, sometimes an effort doesn't work. It indicates that the librarian could retreat but he never surrenders.
4. Changing the attitudes of people is more difficult than changing the technology in a library. A librarian should be flexible while dealing with staff as well as with the library related community. The development of a library is a continuous struggle with patience and tolerance.
5. Effective communication is key to getting the financial, legal and moral support of faculty, administration, and the government. Also, good communication helps a librarian to market the products and services of the library. A librarian cannot depend upon only one method of communication. Sometimes he has to use multiple methods of communication to reach out effectively.

CONCLUSION

The principles I mentioned above are not hard and fast rules for a library leader. The leadership principles and management strategies may vary with the nature, scope, size, and strategic position of a library. More importantly, the management strategy of a librarian depends upon the psychology, nature and behavior of a community in which he serves.

The Application of Leadership and Management Principles and Strategies to a Library and Information Service

P. R. Goswami

SUMMARY. The paper presents an overview of the method and procedure followed by the National Social Science Documentation Centre, India, to assess the present state of affairs relating to publication policy, bibliographical control, distribution and use of government reports in India. The result of an opinion survey on the subject using Delphi technique has been included. The results show that there are gaps in government report collections in libraries. These reports have enormous research value. The underutilization of these reports can be ascribed to both service inadequacies and user motivation. There is an urgent need to compile a comprehensive catalogue of all government reports (published by the states as well as the center) which will eventually take the form of a user's guide. *[Article copies available for a fee from The Haworth Document Delivery Service: 1-800-HAWORTH. E-mail address: <docdelivery@haworthpress.com> Website: <http://www.HaworthPress.com> © 2002 by The Haworth Press, Inc. All rights reserved.]*

KEYWORDS. Government reports, India–social science libraries, Delphi technique, government publications–acquisition

P. R. Goswami is Director, National Social Science Documentation Center, Indian Council of Social Science Research Aruna Asaf Ali Road, New Delhi 110 067 (E-mail: prgoswami@hotmail.com).

[Haworth co-indexing entry note]: "The Application of Leadership and Management Principles and Strategies to a Library and Information Service." Goswami, P. R. Co-published simultaneously in *Science & Technology Libraries* (The Haworth Information Press, an imprint of The Haworth Press, Inc.) Vol. 23, No. 2/3, 2002, pp. 35-42; and: *Leadership and Management Principles in Libraries in Developing Countries* (ed: Wei Wei, Sue O'Neill Johnson, and Sylvia E. A. Piggott) The Haworth Information Press, an imprint of The Haworth Press, Inc., 2002, pp. 35-42. Single or multiple copies of this article are available for a fee from The Haworth Document Delivery Service [1-800-HAWORTH, 9:00 a.m. - 5:00 p.m. (EST). E-mail address: docdelivery@haworthpress.com].

http://www.haworthpress.com/web/STL
© 2002 by The Haworth Press, Inc. All rights reserved.
Digital Object Identifier: 10.1300/J122v23n02_05

Indian Council of Social Science Research (ICSSR) New Delhi is the premier body for the social scientists in India. National Social Science Documentation Centre (NASSDOC) functions as a division of ICSSR. It maintains a research and reference library and provides information support service to researchers who are scattered all over the country. One of the objectives of NASSDOC is to provide document delivery service to scholars who live in small towns. ICSSR also provides maintenance grant to 27 research institutions. NASSDOC library actively collects research documents, which are normally not available in other libraries. One major component of this collection consists of government reports which as we will see are not always 'readily available.' The acquisition policy of NASSDOC says that selective 'government serials and reports' (Centre as well as states) are important and they should be acquired on a regular basis.

However, a general inventory of the NASSDOC library's collection revealed that many reports released by the prominent planning and policy making bodies in India such as those from the Planning Commission, Ministry of Agriculture, Ministry of Commerce, Ministry of Industry, Reserve Bank of India, etc., were missing from the collection. The same is true for agencies such as Central Statistical Organisation (CSO), National Sample Survey Organisation (NSSO), Registrar General of India (RGI), which publish statistical serials on a regular basis. The inventory demonstrated that there are serious gaps in the serials collection within the NASSDOC library. In fact, most of the ICSSR collections consist of uncoordinated and fragmentary selections of government reports. As a result, the collection remains underutilized and as a result the collection has limited research value.

The challenge before the NASSDOC Director was to create a system for 'developing and maintaining a responsive and useful collection of government report for the researchers.' The task was gigantic because all levels of government in India {Union, state, municipal and district} publish a wide array of administration reports, commission and committee reports, survey/census results, expert committee/working group reports in an uncoordinated manner all over the country. And due to the vastness of the country, it is practically impossible to even quantify the number of such reports published in a single year much less identify individual reports.

In order to make a serious analysis of this subject, NASSDOC decided to adopt the Delphi technique. The Delphi technique is a management tool which can be used to predict the future, to assess current needs and to gain expert consensus while at the same time clarifying minority opinions. The Delphi technique is essentially a method of collecting and organizing data comprised of expert opinion. The exact procedure followed can vary depending on the type of study, however we basically used this technique to:

a. Elicit relatively brief statements regarding expected major developments in the field.
b. Share these points of view with other members of the group as well as assess their opinions. Establish an overall set of expectations through consensus.

The ultimate aim of Delphi procedure was to gain consensus on various predictions or statements under consideration. Therefore, if the judgment of the expert panel converges, then the agreement obtained from the group of individual experts can be considered to be a consensus judgment. Once consensus is reached then a plan can be drawn up accordingly.

The Delphi technique has been called the cornerstone of futures' research. It is frequently used to forecast the future. This technique is considered as an efficient and effective group communication process that avoids many of the psychological distractions inherent to round table discussions. This technique is used to systematically elicit judgement from the experts in their areas of specialisation.

Another issue examined by NASSDOC was the development of a government report collection for the social science researchers. The 'Case Study' method was adopted for this purpose. A case study is basically a description of real life situations. It draws on the experience of the participants. Included as participants were librarians familiar with government documents collections, users of reports (i.e., researchers) and heads of publications unit of government agencies. We used the information gathered from this case study to develop the following 'brief statements':

1. Most of the prominent social science libraries in India acquire government reports from agents who deal with official publications.
2. Libraries attached to government departments and institutions directly funded by the government have the privilege of getting complimentary copies of reports through the government's 'free mailing list' system.

3. Agents dealing with government reports supply only those titles which have a price tag and are available through normal trade channels.

4. Most of the committee/commission reports, working group/task force/expert group recommendations and administration reports (i.e., annual report on the working of different government bodies) are un-priced documents and are therefore not available through traditional trade channels.

5. Priced reports are supplied to the libraries on an 'as and when published' basis by the agents.

6. There is a historic absence of reliable publishers' catalogues and this makes it difficult for a library to identify gaps in its collection.

7. The utility of a report is closely intertwined with timeliness of its release. Timeliness means both speed and punctuality. The meaning of speed is that the government reports are made available to the users soon after the period of time to which they refer, where as punctuality means that the reports are made available near to the date of their release, which has been decided and made public in advance.

8. As there is hardly any coordination among the different units of a government body, timeliness factor in release of a report is often not assigned a priority. Many reports are published with a time lag of two to three years.

9. A portion of government reports is published as serials; and gaps are a common feature in most of the libraries. Serials by definition are published in successive parts and intended to continue indefinitely. They are different from monographs for they continue and change. Normally monograph entries stay unchanged once they are made but all characteristics of a serial may alter during its lifetime.

10. There is wastefulness in government publishing. Free mailing lists are maintained on the basis of requests received, and 'priority users' are identified often through the 'seniority' of a person in the organization. As a result, many "high" priority users turn out to be non-users. At the time of their 'transfer' or 'retirement,' government reports are unceremoniously thrown out and sold as 'waste papers.' Because there is no uniformity publishing standard reports do not necessarily have the same paper size, typesetting, titling and binding which means that it is often hard to identify reports.

On the basis of the above statements, expert opinions were obtained from a group of people comprising government document librarians and social science researchers, particularly economists who are avid users of government published reports.

The opinions of experts were obtained mainly through structured interviews. The opinions where then enumerated and categorized. Many of these opinions related to organizational aspects of the government's publication programme. A mission-oriented approach to identify, acquire and increase the use of reports was suggested. The observations and recommendations of experts are summarized below:

a. Librarians managing government reports' collection identified the following categories of reports:

- Administrative Reports
- Statistical Reports
- Commission and Committee Reports
- Research Reports

They said that traditionally government publishes thousands of reports every year. There is no bibliographical control for these compilations at any level of government. A majority of these reports remain confined to the government offices and are never distributed. In fact, diversity of practices in government offices with regard to printing, distribution and announcement of government documents has generated a genuine demand for coordination and integration of bibliographic activities.

b. It was also observed by the experts that most of the reports are distributed among priority users with the help of a mailing list. Maintenance and revision of a mailing list is normally done by a junior level official. As a result, analysis or judgment is not applied to what names are placed on the list. This means that potential users of a report may not get an opportunity to consult it. During the 1970s and 1980s many government publications were indiscriminately marked as 'for official use' or 'for restricted circulation.' The public dissemination units of government agencies are currently in a dormant state. There is an urgent need to launch an awareness campaign to increase the distribution and use of government reports. Users' group from academic institutions and research units must be associated with this campaign.

c. The experts also held the view that there has been a shift in policy. Government of India's Central Secretariat Manual of Office Procedure (1996) now says that the restrictive classification 'for official use only' will not be assigned to any printed report, pamphlet, or compilation unless it contains information which would not be in the public interest to disclose. In view of the present state of affairs relating to dissemination of government generated information, it would be worthwhile to consider a proposal for a depository programme for official publications under direct control of Department of Culture, Government of India, which is the premier body for planning and development of library and information services in the country. The proposed depository programme would have all legal powers to ensure that the access to information sources like reports reach potential users.

d. The experts also said that information technology (IT) can play a crucial role in organizing and streamlining the dissemination process of government reports. National Informatics Centre (NIC) which functions under the aegis of Government of India, which has developed web-based services for many government departments. A few of these departments have put their flagship reports on their web sites. The declining cost of data storage and communication has led to an explosion in the volume of available information. Many government agencies are now willing to explore the possibility of providing e-text of government reports against nominal fees. This can substantially reduce the time lag in publication of reports.

e. The experts emphasized the need for collecting exhaustive bibliographical details of reports. In case of serial publications, detailed bibliographical history is needed because in most of the government serials, the title of the responsible body (i.e., author) undergoes changes during their lifetime. Also, it is necessary to compile an annual catalogue of all categories of government published reports. The catalogue should include details such as the procedure for acquiring official publications. This catalog should also include a users' guide for publications like budget documents and sample survey reports are also urgently needed. With the help of such a guide, one can get a better understanding of structure and content of these publications; including concepts and definitions used.

As a national body, NASSDOC has started an all out effort to build a comprehensive collection of official reports. The creation of a liaison with publication units of prominent planning and policy-making units has been assigned top priority. And the officials working in these units are being sensitized so that they can appreciate the research value of these reports. A survey of users has revealed that there is a need to increase usage of these reports. Also there is a need for proper documentation of concepts, definitions, and terms used in the text of the reports. The concept 'service marketing' is now emphasized in the organizational culture of NASSDOC. As a marketer, NASSDOC makes promises and builds expectations for its services. The famous law of library science propounded by Dr. Ranganathan is now gaining ground at NASSDOC. It is 'every reader his report' and 'every report its reader.' The staff members now believe that the only criteria that should count when evaluating library services are those defined by library users because only users can accurately judge quality. All other judgments are irrelevant.

Following lessons have been learnt from this mission-oriented project, which was undertaken by the NASSDOC:

1. Government reports have enormous research value. The under-utilization of these reports can be ascribed to both service inadequacies and lack of user motivation.
2. Nowadays, most of the training programmes are designed to make librarians conversant with IT applications. In order to achieve excellence in service, librarians are required to be information sensitive. Training should be designed in a way so that librarians are able to understand and evaluate esoteric sources of information (e.g., Report on Consumer Expenditure).
3. Experiential learning (i.e., learning by doing) has a greater role to play for reference librarians working in the government reports section. Intuitive judgment is a product of experience. Intuition depends on the experience to recognize key patterns that indicate the dynamics of the situation.
4. In a special library or in a unit of a library having special collection (like government reports), professionals working in the reference/circulation desk play a vital role in enhancing the value of the services. They create and maintain users' satisfaction. As contact persons, they perform external representation function, and they possess important information about users' preferences.

The project is still underway at the NASSDOC. It is expected that within a period of two years, all important government reports and serials will be acquired in collaboration with Central Secretariat Library, Department of Culture, Government of India. A comprehensive catalogue of all government reports (published by the state as well as the centre) is under preparation. It will eventually take the form of a users' guide for the researchers in social sciences.

REFERENCES

Menezes, Francis A. Cases in management. New Delhi, Tata McGraw Hill, 1981.
Zeithmal, Valerie A. Delivering quality service: balancing customer perceptions and expectations. New York, The Free Press, 1990.

Application of Leadership
and Management Principles for Libraries:
Some Reflections from India

V. K. J. Jeevan

SUMMARY. This paper will present some of the developments in providing refined information services and better information organization such as the electronic SDI service and in-house library software development work in the library of a premier academic institute in India. It will also stress activities concerned with professional development and growth such as experiences gained as part of the technical committee in a national level conference, activities as moderator of IFLA's listserver for Library & Information Science in India (INDIA-LIS), and work related to LIS education. The paper also describes some aspects of the future plan, of evolving a content personalization system with the aid of electronic contents procured through subscriptions and consortia access as well as free resources on the Web. *[Article copies available for a fee from The Haworth Document Delivery Service: 1-800-HAWORTH. E-mail address: <docdelivery@haworth press.com> Website: <http://www.HaworthPress.com> © 2002 by The Haworth Press, Inc. All rights reserved.]*

V. K. J. Jeevan is Assistant Librarian, Indian Institute of Technology, Kharagpur, West Bengal 721 302 India (E-mail: vkjj@rediffmail.com).

[Haworth co-indexing entry note]: "Application of Leadership and Management Principles for Libraries: Some Reflections from India." Jeevan, V. K. J. Co-published simultaneously in *Science & Technology Libraries* (The Haworth Information Press, an imprint of The Haworth Press, Inc.) Vol. 23, No. 2/3, 2002, pp. 43-55; and: *Leadership and Management Principles in Libraries in Developing Countries* (ed: Wei Wei, Sue O'Neill Johnson, and Sylvia E. A. Piggott) The Haworth Information Press, an imprint of The Haworth Press, Inc., 2002, pp. 43-55. Single or multiple copies of this article are available for a fee from The Haworth Document Delivery Service [1-800-HAWORTH, 9:00 a.m. - 5:00 p.m. (EST). E-mail address: docdelivery@haworthpress.com].

http://www.haworthpress.com/web/STL
© 2002 by The Haworth Press, Inc. All rights reserved.
Digital Object Identifier: 10.1300/J122v23n02_06

KEYWORDS. Indian Institute of Technology (IIT) Kharagpur, INDEST consortium, electronic SDI, Library Automation and Manpower Project (LAMP), library automation software, Central Library Automation Software (CLAS), Database Management Systems (DBMS), Information Management in e-Libraries (IMeL), INDIA-LIS, content personalization, distance education in library & information science [India], Continuing Education Programmes (CEP)

INTRODUCTION

The Indian Institute of Technology (IIT), Kharagpur, founded in 1951 as an autonomous body and premier academic institute by the Government of India, is devoted to high quality human resources development in science and technology [1]. It is the first, biggest and most diversified among the seven such Institutes located in different parts of the country. The institute enrolls nearly 3,000 students, 450 faculty and another 1,500 technical, research and administrative staff. The Central Library (CL) of the institute occupies a unique place in the academic activities of over 25 departments, center and schools, by serving their library and information needs. The collection contains over 400,000 volumes consisting of books, journals, microforms, standards, theses, reports, maps, and electronic information media.

The Central Library commenced the use of computer systems in 1987 and automation activities gained momentum in 1993. The orientation of the library had been solely in the manual mode up to the late '80s and was a mix of manual and automated in the '90s. The new century has seen substantial reduction in manual procedures. The library catalogue is available in digital form and the Online Public Access Catalogue (OPAC) can be accessed through the campus Intranet and Internet from its web site [2]. The Library also publishes lists of current additions of books and journals on a fortnightly basis. To supplement the journal collection and to provide timely information services, a facility called Electronic Library comprising electronic databases, a few multimedia PCs and relevant software along with video media was established in 1994. Presently, the CL is one of the largest and fully automated technical libraries in the country with many resources available online, a modern electronic library, CD-ROM networking (through jukebox-tower as well as by copying to servers with high capacity hard disc and assorted software), and fiber optic (ATM) LAN with VSAT connectivity. The INDEST consortium [3] for major publicly funded technical institutions has substantially increased the availability of bibliographic and full text information resources from late 2002/early 2003.

ELECTRONIC SDI SERVICE

The Central Library of IIT Kharagpur started alerting faculty members (around 500 in number) about current literature on new developments in their chosen field of specialization in May 1997. The controlled vocabulary used by the indexing and abstracting services is also useful for personal profiles. The construction of these profiles according to the standardized terms is a highly intellectual job and a constant monitoring mechanism of the service was evolved out of useful feedback and constructive comments. These profiles were matched for relevant literature on a few frequently updated science and technology databases, and the matching results with bibliographic information and abstract were sent through e-mail with a request to users to furnish their comments on the utility and relevance. Based on the monthly feedback through e-mail and phone about the articles' relevance from the SDI output, with suggestions to alter or add keywords, an optimum level of recall and precision had been ensured by constant interaction with the users and by applying the various permutations and combinations of keywords.

This service fulfills the twin purposes of alerting the users to the latest research published in their research field and also of providing sufficient inspiration to acquire the relevant article(s) either by photocopy or through other resource sharing arrangement [4]. This service enables the library staff to ascertain subject specializations of its faculty and to convert them as per the controlled vocabulary of the database which was a good learning exercise in content based information retrieval. Also this enabled faculty members to save considerable time in sifting through the mass of current information. We operated the service for around two years and then discontinued it due to factors such as complexities in mapping inter-intra disciplinary research information profiles, the differences in information scanning by intermediaries and researchers, demand for full text rather than bibliographic information, and manpower problems. We are working on providing a new look to this service by content personalization, as discussed in a later part of this paper.

IN-HOUSE AUTOMATION SOFTWARE

Though the CL commenced the use of computer systems in 1987, the automation activities gathered momentum only in 1993 and much headway in these activities was made through the Library Automation and Manpower Project (LAMP) taken up with the help of some research projects offered to CL [5]. All library housekeeping operations like acquisition of books, card printing, circulation, and so forth are done through the commercial automation software (commercialware) purchased in 1994. The library OPAC provides information about over 400,000 books and other reading materials such as back volumes of journals, theses, standards, microforms, and so forth. Achieving such a target a decade back was a unique feat even at the national level.

The library automation software is different from many other ready-to-use commercial software/electronic products procured in a library. The software supplied by the software developer is to be fed with data concerning local collection, patrons, library rules, etc., before starting service through the same in different sections of the library. Thus relevant software for a particular library has to be evaluated from various angles such as suitability of the software for the target library, its existing clients, hardware and operating systems supported, computer awareness among staff and users, network as well as computer infrastructure in the Institution, and above all the cost and after-sales support. Any commercialware for that matter developed for a general library (without any target library in consideration) has to be customized effectively for the individual library [6].

In the CL, even after eight years of working with the commercialware, the penetration of complete automation has been quite mixed as customizing a commercialware is an involved process. The book related sections of Acquisition, Processing and Circulation were better customized in the commercialware whereas the journal sections found refuge in a mix of packages as customization of these sections wasn't realized much largely due to the software, administrative and personnel problems.

The crucial and perennial problems that we encountered while working with the commercialware include extra charges for platform changes and server upgrades, difficulty in effective customization of all the modules, discrepancy with respect to system requirements suggested and actually required, delays in responses to the user's commands, insufficient training to local system analysts, absence of Relational Database Management Systems (RDBMS) and Application Programming Interfaces (APIs), distracting user interface, rigidity in menus and discouraging customer support. Our evaluation of the currently used and many other commercial packages available in the country in terms of features, support and monetary involvement prompted the CL to design and develop a robust and reliable library automation package to minimize the lacunas with the existing package and to maximize full advantages of an electronic and web enabled environment [7, 8].

With the help of a few project staff, the CL has successfully completed the implementation of the library automation software, Central Library Automation System (CLAS) to handle all the housekeeping tasks concerned with procuring, processing, and servicing information resources [9]. The software is undergoing testing and will have the features to communicate with all the stake holders in a library system through electronic means and will have a web enabled interface with capability for future additions like automated security system and the centralized administration software. Two HP 9000 A 180 C servers were procured, to keep one server on the private network of library for database operations by library staff, and the other for mirrored OPAC serving on the campus Intranet and Internet. To have safe and secure network services on the campus Intranet, the UNIX operating system is preferred over Windows.

Since automatic power on and booting up in the event of power breakdown and UPS failure in the night, the HP Ux (Version 11.0) operating system was preferred. Oracle was selected as the database engine for its preferred virtues and also due to its wide distribution and support, and for the better support of web enabled tools like WebDB, which is used as the front-end. To have a secure database server where users use the server for 24 hours and the Library is open only for 14 hours, configuring a mirror catalogue server is most important. Two possibilities existed to do mirroring, one at the OS level using UNIX features and another at the DBMS level with the aid of Oracle tools. Since we found the second option convenient and cost less on system resources, it is being used for real time OPAC serving, even though we successfully explored the first option also.

Though this development was undertaken basically for the exclusive use of the CL, we have interests to generalize this package for other similar academic and special libraries in the country interested in such a package. The generalization may involve not only modification of the software routines but also changes in operating system and database engine.

TECHNICAL WORK IN IMeL

To mark the Golden Jubilee of IIT Kharagpur and to celebrate the "Year of Books" declared by the Government of India, the CL organized the National Conference on Information Management in e-Libraries (IMeL) on February 26-27, 2002. The call for papers was circulated in printed and electronic form to major libraries and Institutions in India well in advance of the conference on the following themes:

- Information Storage Retrieval and Services
- Distributed/Networked Information Systems
- Digital Libraries
- Database Management
- IPR/Legal Aspects and Future Trends
- User Education, System Evaluation and Surveys
- Consortia and Resource Sharing
- Engineering and Technical Libraries
- Policies, Standards and Practices

Information about the submission of papers and other details of the conference was also kept on the web sites of CL and Institute. Accordingly, we received an encouraging response from professionals throughout the length and breadth of the country. Eighty-six papers were received including the text of three invited lectures. Many of the authors interacted frequently through mail and most of their queries were answered on the same day. A detailed list of reviewers was identified by applying criteria such as publications, place of work, major contributions to the profession, and above all their interest in supporting the review. Hard copies of each of the papers were sent to one reviewer in the eastern part of the country where the Institute is located and one to outside, and some of the papers were modified by the author as per reviewer's comments. Many other papers were finalized without modification due to paucity of time. All the papers selected were categorized as per the subject matter into various themes listed above and sent for publication to a private publisher located in New Delhi. The 650 page proceedings [10] was completed and delivered to our site three days before the conference, well ahead of the locally printed 60 page souvenir.

The CD-ROM version of the Proceedings was prepared and published internally by the CL. In addition another action item for the technical committee was to schedule the invited papers, contributed papers (held in parallel sessions), and product presentations in different sessions in the two day conference. Over 160 participants attended the conference and many of our delegates expressed appreciation for how IMeL was different from other library conferences in India. Perhaps one area which made a remarkable difference was the technical component of the conference, a well balanced mix of contributed papers and invited lectures by experts in the country, as well as the printed and electronic version of the proceedings of the conference supplied to the participants.

INDIA-LIS

INDIA-LIS is the third listserv started in India [11] in the field of library and information science, after the LIS-FORUM [12] by the National Centre for Science Information, Indian Institute of Science, Bangalore and IASLIC-LIST [13] from Indian Association of Special Libraries and Information Centres, Kolkata, and perhaps the only international one even today. IFLANET was willing to sponsor a LIS-INDIA list on their machine at the National Library of Canada and the CL approached them in 1998/99 and then the collaboration came along with the hosting of INDIA-LIS. The content of the discussions on the list together with the administrative aspects like granting/cancellation of membership will be the responsibility of the moderator from India whereas the system related responsibilities would be met by IFLA.

Currently IFLA's lists including INDIA-LIS have been shifted from the National Library of Canada to INIST, France [14]. The list actively discusses the present state of affairs of library and librarians in India, along with quick dissemination of information about events like workshops, courses, conferences and job openings in the field. Now there are at least a dozen mailing lists concerning the library profession in the country and many new ones are starting. INDIA-LIS strives to maintain its uniqueness by always searching for and disseminating fresh content.

CONTENT PERSONALIZATION

Content Personalization is proposed as a future activity we may be taken up in the near future and is very similar but broader in scope to the activities performed by the library for Current Awareness Services (CAS) and Selective Dissemination of Information (SDI) services. A major difference in the case of personalization is the attempt to map and provide full text information rather than mere surrogates like indexes or abstracts in the case of CAS/SDI. The basic reasons behind Content Personalization in a library must be:

- Large amounts of content procured are unused
- A small part of content acquired are not being used properly
- Difficulty of attracting the users and satisfying their demands
- Electronic contents available can be easily personalized
- Efficient collection management
- Improve the image of Library

Still reasons like importance not felt, lack of infrastructure/cooperation from Management, and inadequate funds/staff may prevent personalizing library contents. Most of the time, this may lead to information under-use which will have a drastic impact on the research and development output, as the right sources may not reach the right person at the right time. However, there are certain attempts from portals, libraries and information suppliers to personalize their content repository to individual users. NewsAgent for Libraries, a project funded by the Electronic Libraries Programme (eLib) in the UK, (URL: http://newsagent.ukoln.ac.uk) is a user configurable electronic news and current awareness service for library and information professionals [15]. The Personal Digital Library (PDL), from the Electronic Library Project at De Montfort University, Leicester, UK (ELINOR) is a personal information system which acts as a front end to other electronic library systems [16].

The 'Digital Portfolio Archives' (DPAs) project at University of California, Los Angeles (UCLA) allows teachers to build a personalized information system or DPAs; and enables students to incorporate the components of the teacher's DPA and additional project-related materials into their own DPAs [17]. MyLibrary is a Cornell University Library initiative to provide personalized library services such as MyLinks, a tool for collecting and organizing resources for private use by a patron, and MyUpdates, a tool to help scholars stay informed of new resources provided by the library [18]. Another MyLibrary (URL: http://my.lib. ncsu.edu/) project is operational at the North Carolina State University (NCSU) Libraries which is a user-centered front-end to collection of Internet and information resources and provides a customizable interface to several types of information.

The key elements of a Content Personalization System (CPS) are user interest management systems, electronic content servers, and a network or medium to access the tailored contents [19].

USER INTEREST MANAGEMENT SUBSYSTEM

User interest will be collected through forms, library usage or through machine learning.

Online/Offline Forms: In the past, printed forms were circulated to elicit the subject specialization of users before venturing into an SDI service. Nowadays, the same information can be collected from web forms, and the process can be made interactive by enabling the user to modify terms based on the results retrieved.

Library Usage History: The usage by individual user can be explored to refine their subject profiles such as what kind of books or journals they are browsing in library, issuing out/Xeroxing from library, requested for resource sharing/interlibrary loan, citing in their articles, etc.

Artificial Intelligence: AI techniques may be employed to auto-learn and intelligently refine the subject specialization of the individual client.

The user interests collected will be incorporated into a suitable database engine and access will be provided to users in a restrictive fashion so that a person can modify his/her profile as and when needed without the intervention of library professionals. However, care should be taken about not disclosing another person's profile to a user, so that what he/she can browse is only some schematic or pattern of group interests. Profiles will be constructed at an individual and group level to render different types of services. This may go through different iterations and refinements based on feedback as well as outputs of searches with respect to profile. Since information retrieval works based on the search terms selected, and for profile based matching, it is necessary to identify the essential concepts of the subject specialization of the users and there should be correspondence between key words and index resources. We are planning to create individual pages on the CPS server to map specializations and fields of interest of all teachers and researchers of the Institute.

ELECTRONIC CONTENT SERVER SUBSYSTEM

The contents for personalization must include easily available electronic information such as e-journals and electronic databases, but must also use full text databases, book floppies/CDs, Internet/Web resources, and scanned/digitized printed text. Information in electronic form currently resides in different servers in the library like bibliographic data of the holdings in the library automation server for housekeeping operations, CD-ROM servers for access to electronic databases in CD form, web servers for intranet/Internet information, and so forth.

The INDEST consortium has significantly increased the information access base in IIT libraries and the CL has been able to access prominent science and technology information resources such as IEL, ScienceDirect and IDEAL, SpringerLink, ABI/INFORM, ACM Digital Library, and bibliographic sources such as COMPENDEX, INSPEC, SciFinder Scholar and ISI-Thomson Web of Science. Apart from this, many of the subscribed society journals are also accessible in electronic form from the publisher's web sites. Some of these publishers permit local archiving of these resources which will facilitate amassing substantial amounts of information resources in the content servers of CL. These servers will also search relevant information from the Web based on specific requests. Since many libraries in India are planning for digital libraries in the near future, planning a distributed approach will yield better results than a unitary system. Internet, web, database technology and their interfacing is leading to interesting experiences of data storage, organization and demand based retrieval.

NETWORK/DELIVERY SUBSYSTEM

An efficient CPS system will interface with one or more content servers in a distributed environment to extract contents of interest and concern to individual users. They may use the proprietary search engines of individual systems or use the CPS search engine. The contents retrieved by the personalization system may be delivered as daily/ weekly/monthly email alerts with links to full text sources. Another less intrusive possibility is to create web pages for individual users (with password to access them) on the server itself and they will be notified of updates in such pages occasionally. The CPS will essentially provide two types of results, one exact (private) match based on the person's specialization and another related (group) match based on the department/research area the person is working with options to browse either.

LIS EDUCATION AND TRAINING

The student profile of distance education programmes in LIS can be broadly classified into two types, graduates working in library without formal library training, and the vast majority is the fresh graduates who were not able to secure admission in a regular library school [20]. Another area of utmost concern is the pass percentage of distance learners. It seems as though a large number of students have been enrolled with much fanfare, be it the seriousness of learners, or the pedagogy, only a smaller percentage than that of regular students were victorious. The supply and demand supply theory is not in vogue for human resource development in the country unfortunately due to the large population, massive spread of education and the democratic ideals practiced.

The major job giver, the government institutions, are not recruiting as early due to downsizing, re-orientation of new professionals with diverse skills for information work, and what's happening now is the mere substitution of old posts rather than generation of new jobs. The information work is still handled in a big way as a stopgap arrangement by clerical/office staff, in a large number of private industrial and commercial firms [21]. With a considerable number of regular courses plus a continuous rise in distance courses catered a manifold increase in the number of library degree recipients over the jobs generated every year. It may also be noted that library degree holders are unable to find suitable placements outside the country like engineering or medical professionals, due to various reasons, such as poor international orientation or overemphasis on localization in library courses in the country, job market hostile training, feeble academic competence of learners, etc. [20].

Since the way and rate at which information is generated, organized and used is witnessing rapid changes in recent times, a discipline like LIS meant to tackle the intricacies of the information for societal development will not be taught effectively and practiced perfectly by exposing to a framed curriculum during one's formal education. The discipline is embracing other disciplines like computers, communication technology, cognition research, etc., to provide right answers to the problems caused by the emerging information infrastructure. It is imperative for the information practitioners to continuously monitor and augment their skills to deal with 'pinpointed information from the deluge.' Manual means of tackling information will not help the user/professional to solve emerging problems in the actual research setup and the present day researchers expect a quick response time from their colleagues in the information profession. Such skills can only be instilled by constituting Continuing Education Programmes (CEP) for Library Professionals.

There are essentially two objectives of CEP for information professionals, one is to update their skills to perform better in the routine and day-to-day jobs, and another is to revamp their professional and intellectual commitment by equipping them with specialized knowledge [22]. Thus the distance education facilities should frame IT intensive short and long term courses to meet the continuing education needs of the professionals, to perform effectively in a largely service oriented and dynamically evolving discipline, rather than duplicating formal courses. A symbiosis between formal and informal education could also be established then. Most of the topics to be dealt as part of CE pertain to the latest developments in computerized information handling, thus needing considerable elaboration and numerous hands-on trials to inculcate the requisite skills, and are difficult to achieve completely in short term courses.

The plus points put forward in favour of distance education such as no dislocation from job and other formalities, convenient education at one's space and pace, etc., must further enable the CE activities to broadly propagate. Most of the distance education providers have courses at various levels on computers and IT and entered into partnership arrangements with computer firms to provide practical training for these courses. They can take a lead in offering both short and long term CE courses and modules for information professionals by using these facilities and identifying suitable topics of interest to current information processing and services [21].

CONCLUSION

In the present time, it is not the best but the smart who survive, and many management and leadership principles fail in practice. Also, the people who are more vocal can usurp leadership without contributing seriously to the welfare of the organization. There are also external interference and sociopolitical aspects concerning the running of any organization. The activities mentioned above have made a difference by identifying the major professional elements intertwined in each one of them and by delivering efficient and effective services in a unique fashion. It is through this difference and commitment to our professional cause, hard work, and always keeping track of international and national developments that we are planning to make an impact on managerial effectiveness and leadership.

REFERENCES

1. http://www.iitkgp.ernet.in/.
2. http://www.library.iitkgp.ernet.in.
3. http://www.library.iitb.ac.in/indest/.
4. Jeevan, V K J, "Info Alert Facility for Research (IAFR): An Indian Attempt," *New Library World*, MCB Press, UK, 100(1152), 1999, pp. 315-318.

5. Jeevan, V K J, "Kharagpur Electronic Library on the Internet (KELNET)" *Library Hi-Tech*, 18(3), 2000, pp. 272-278.

6. Jeevan, V K J, "In-house Library Software Development at IIT Kharagpur: Opportunities and Challenges," International CALIBER 2003, Ahmedabad, Nirma Education and Research Foundation, 13-15 February 2003, Conference Volume–Mapping Technology on Libraries and People, Ahmedabad: INFLIBNET, 2003, pp. 140-152.

7. Jeevan, V K J, "Design and Development of a Library Automation System Using Oracle 8I," M.Tech Thesis, Indian Institute of Technology Kharagpur, 2001, 90 p.

8. Jeevan, V K J and Raja Kumar, R V, "Design of Indigenous Library Automation Software: Experiences of the Central Library, IIT Kharagpur, Information Management in e-Libraries" Proceedings of the National Conference on Information Management in e-Libraries (IMeL), New Delhi, Allied, 2002, pp. 401-410.

9. Kumar, Bharath K. et al., "Central Library Automation Software (CLAS): A Library Software, Information Management in e-Libraries" Proceedings of the National Conference on Information Management in e-Libraries (IMeL), New Delhi: Allied, 2002, pp. 411-418.

10. National Conference of Information Management in e-Libraries (IMeL), Proceedings of the National Conference on Information Management in e-Libraries (IMeL), organized by the Central Library, IIT Kharagpur, ed. by S. Parthan and V. K. J. Jeevan, New Delhi: Allied Publishers, ISBN: 81-7764-279-0, 2002, xv, 650 p.

11. Jeevan, V K J, "India-LIS: A New e-Mail Forum for Indian Infocrats," *University News*, 37(45), Nov. 8, 1999, pp. 6-10.

12. Meenaxi Gulla, T.B. Rajashekar and A Sreenivasa Ravi: LIS-FORUM: Electronic Mail Discussion Forum for Library & Information Services, Information Today & Tomorrow (NISSAT Newsletter), 14(1), 1995, pp. 25-26.13. *IASLIC Newsletter*, February, Calcutta: IASLIC, 1998, p. 3.

14. http://infoserv.inist.fr/wwsympa.fcgi/info/india-lis.

15. Tedd, L. A., Yeates, R. A Personalised Current Awareness Service for Library and Information Services Staff: An Overview of the NewsAgent for Libraries Project, *Program*, 32 (4) Oct 1998, pp. 373-90.

16. Zhao, D. The Personal Digital Library, ELINOR: Electronic Library Project. London: Bowker-Saur for British Library, 1998, pp. 97-103.

17. Gilliland-Swetland, A., The Digital Portfolio Archives Project, California University at Los Angeles, Department of Library and Information Science, 1997.

18. Cohen, Suzanne et al. MyLibrary: Personalized Electronic Services in the Cornell University Library, *D-Lib Magazine*, 6(4), April 2000, http://www.dlib.org/dlib/april00/mistlebauer/04mistlebauer.html.

19. Jeevan, V K J, Padhi, P, "Towards Personalising the Electronic Contents in Technical Libraries," *University News*, 40(21), May 27-June 2, 2002, pp. 3-9.

20. Jeevan, V K J, "Distance or Distress Education for Librarianship," *Herald of Library Science*, 37(3-4), July-Oct 1998, pp. 196-204.

21. Jeevan, V K J, "Open and Distance Learning for Library Science Professionals," *University News*, 40(16), Apr 22-28, 2002, pp. 3-9.

22. Jeevan, V K J, "Continuing Education of Information Professionals in India: A Model Using Open Universities," *FID Review*, Netherlands, 1 (2/3), pp. 34-38, 1999.

Traditional Values Still Relevant in Library Usage and Readership Enhancement: Challenges Before a Librarian

K. A. Raju

SUMMARY. In most developing countries, the effectiveness of a special library is still measured based on the collection and its usage in quantitative terms. Managing a library is not what it was a decade ago, as the impact of automation and raising expectations of users and management with the emergence of Internet are all adding to the tensions and anxieties of the modern day librarian. A learning programme on Library Utilization and Readership Enhancement (LURE), an innovative experiment, conducted at several intervals in the 1990s at the National Institute of Rural Development, Hyderabad, India, was presented as an illustration. Through LURE, the interaction with users of the library and peers in the profession increased and the library services improved. The strategies for long-term adoption were identified and presented. *[Article copies available for a fee from The Haworth Document Delivery Service: 1-800-HAWORTH. E-mail address: <docdelivery@haworthpress.com> Website: <http://www.HaworthPress.com> © 2002 by The Haworth Press, Inc. All rights reserved.]*

KEYWORDS. Library management, library automation, library usage, user participation, management strategies, case study, National Institute of Rural Development

---

K. A. Raju is Director (CORD), National Institute of Rural Development, Rajendranagar, Hyderabad-500 030 (E-mail: karaju@nird.gov.in).

[Haworth co-indexing entry note]: "Traditional Values Still Relevant in Library Usage and Readership Enhancement: Challenges Before a Librarian." Raju, K. A. Co-published simultaneously in *Science & Technology Libraries* (The Haworth Information Press, an imprint of The Haworth Press, Inc.) Vol. 23, No. 2/3, 2002, pp. 57-65; and: *Leadership and Management Principles in Libraries in Developing Countries* (ed: Wei Wei, Sue O'Neill Johnson, and Sylvia E. A. Piggott) The Haworth Information Press, an imprint of The Haworth Press, Inc., 2002, pp. 57-65. Single or multiple copies of this article are available for a fee from The Haworth Document Delivery Service [1-800-HAWORTH, 9:00 a.m. - 5:00 p.m. (EST). E-mail address: docdelivery@haworthpress.com].

Digitial Object Identifier: 10.1300/J122v23n02_07

INTRODUCTION

The importance of any library as a resource center and as a center for continuous learning need not be overemphasized. It has been the experience of many a library, especially a special library attached to an organization in developing countries, that the collection and its use in quantitative terms, often becomes the measure of its affectivity. Maintaining a library today is not like what it was a decade ago as reflected in the literature of the last decade about the changes that are coming in the organization and administration of libraries and the pressures affecting the role of a librarian, to fulfill the demands of the top management as well as its users (Sabaratnam, 1995; Vavrek, 1998; Wormell, 1997). There are instances to show that internal library matters demand more time of the librarians and the technological advances are forcing the librarians to be more proactive than hitherto. With new information technologies, satellite communication systems, intellectual property rights, networking, Internet, etc., the environment in which a modern library operates is becoming more and more complex. Added to these, the budgetary constraints, inadequate infrastructure, falling standards of human resources are compelling the librarian to change his management style from a mere custodian of information to that of a facilitator, a mentor, to bring in corporate culture together with a competitive strategy. Also, the rising expectations of the user and the management, the internal and external environment, and client relationships are all adding to the tensions and anxiety of the modern day librarian.

CASE OF NIRD

Let us examine the case of the library of National Institute of Rural Development (NIRD), Hyderabad, an apex research, training and consultancy organization in India established in 1958. Over the years the modest library was transformed slowly into a resource center for information on rural development, with some reputation. A new name and an identity were given to the library as Center on Rural Documentation (CORD) and a byline "Information Clearinghouse" for Rural Development to give it a corporate image and also a Director was appointed as the Chief in 1990, to steer CORD into a resonating center for excellence in development, information collection and dissemination.

Basically, a library being a service institution, it is recognized that a close interaction between the information providers, processors and users may be necessary to enhance its effectiveness as an information resource center. While we were trying to build up a tempo, somewhere along the line we had a feeling that the users of our library were not coming along with us. This feeling led us into an introspection, which gave rise to a learning programme on Library Utilization and Readership Enhancement (LURE).

LURE-I

Programme LURE-I was to provide a forum for users of the library and the personnel working in the library to come together, to understand each others way of dealing with information, and how the various information barriers can later be overcome to identify the best practices to be followed or to be adopted to increase the utilization of the library resources. This programme, conducted in 1991, was based on the premise of the management that huge amounts of money to equip the library with relevant reading material was provided year after year, and appropriate investments in personnel and infrastructure were made which was not commensurate with the use they were put to (Raju 1991). Therefore the learning programme not only provided an opportunity for interaction between the library professionals and the users but also threw up several practices that are followed in information collection, collation and dissemination which appear to be not very conducive for promoting library utilization or for optimal exploitation of the library resources.

The one day brainstorming session offered a set of simple but effective steps to increase the library use with suggestions like involvement of users in procurement of literature, initiating client based services, etc. The other major recommendations included: (a) Book selection and reacquisition are both important and user participation in both these activities will improve library utilization; (b) User education and user surveys have to be frequently conducted by the library to improve the interaction between users and the library personnel; (c) A brochure on the library highlighting the library collection, cataloging and classification system followed and the services offered would be more useful; (d) Immediate computerization of all activities of the library; (e) Creation of new services like abstracting, alerting service, personalized reference service and making digests on specific topics, etc., may have to be attempted; (f) Augmentation of facilities for document supply and other physical facilities like proper sign boards, stools to reach higher shelves, etc., and (g) Strengthening of the resource sharing at the local level.

These recommendations were taken seriously as they were particularly innovative in the overall development of the library utilization. Fortunately, most of the suggestions could be implemented with a telling effect on the library usage.

Simple activities like book racks free from dust, provision of carrels for exclusive reading, alphabetical display of journals dispensing with subject-wise display, and creation of a separate reading room for journals were some of the improvements in physical facilities made based on the recommendations of LURE-I. A Library Committee comprising senior and junior faculty of the Institute was constituted to improve participatory procurement of library material. A brochure on CORD, its activities, services and perspectives was brought for distribution to the visitors of the library. The major recommendation on the automation of the library using LIBSYS, a software developed by an Indian firm, was taken up in 1992 and the total collection of over 50,000 books and an equal number of journal articles indexed from 1970 onwards, was made available as a database. The entire operation was given to a local private firm, including the retrospective conversion, which was completed within a period of six months so that the CORD library became one of the first few special libraries in the country that was fully automated.

LURE-II

With the completion of the library automation, in 1993 a second programme on LURE was conducted; this time with a difference. The impetus came from the management of the parent organization. There was a constant refrain from the management that with automation is there any improvement in the utilization of library resources? How many faculties are visiting the library? What is the ratio between faculty and participants of various training programmers that visit the library? What special arrangements were made to familiarize the participants with the automation? Also, with computerization of library procedures, a new barrier is likely to be perceived by the users. Such 'automation anxiety' may have to be taken into consideration in designing training programmes on library orientation. Accordingly, the participants for LURE-II were chosen from not only the users of the library but also the participants of the then running courses at the institute, and also some of the librarians of neighboring institutions. This was done for cross-fertilization of ideas and to identify best practices in their organizations.

Several suggestions emerged based on the discussions in the two-day programme, some of which are as follows: (a) promotion of the library with a professional image is essential; (b) library staff should be trained in inter-personnel communication skills; (c) there is a need to display current journals in a more attractive and useful manner like displaying latest issues at a prominent place, in alphabetical sequence, etc.; (d) NIRD publications should be displayed prominently for outside visitors; (e) a marketing approach to its library and information products is essential. For this purpose a library counter and surrounding areas should be used for the display of not only acquired publications but also NIRD publications; (f) there are about 3,000 participants in a year coming to NIRD to participate in the training programmes, who should be given an orientation tour to the library for a better appreciation of its resources; (g) a session on information resources, and information management relevant to the theme of any course wherever possible, should be arranged apart from the display of the publications pertaining to the training programme; (h) a faculty directory, a user manual, continuous training of users and staff on information technology, etc., are other suggestions that emerged from the programme.

After LURE-II, there was a marked improvement in the appreciation of library services, the physical facilities and the environment in the library. Non-book material like CD-ROMs, videos, electronic journals have slowly started to show their presence. In the mid '90s, the Internet opened gates to the information sources world wide, and made possible access to information from a remote location. As a result it has become more important to look into the problems of transforming a traditional library into an information clearinghouse using the developments in information technologies.

LURE-III

Against this backdrop, a third LURE programme was conducted in the year 1998 for three days, after a gap of five years. This learning programme was made into a National Workshop inviting papers from all over India on various themes such as library utilization, techniques of readership enhancement, evaluation of library services, Internet and changing role of the librarian, etc. (NIRD, 1998).

Participants from several parts of the country made their presentations based on their own back-home experience in user education and the identification of user needs. This workshop revealed various kinds of experiments that are on going in different regions of the country by innovative librarians for the best practices that could be identified and demystifying the Internet for the librarian and the user. Two very important and far-reaching recommendations of the workshop were (1) to create a virtual library on rural development to cater to the information needs of the developments community spread throughout the vast country, India, and (2) to use the developments in ICTs in empowering the rural poor and to bridge the digital divide as per the mandate of NIRD.

INNOVATIVE PROGRAMMES

As a follow-up to LURE-III, two innovations were introduced by CORD. One is an internal programme called "Computerized Library & Information Clearing House" (CLIC) charged to develop a 'Gateway of Information on Rural Development' and the other is an outreach programme of bringing the developments in ICTs to the doorsteps of the grass-root level public in the villages. Both are in keeping with the mandate of CORD. The creation of Gateway relates to a continuous database build up using Internet and other resources in the form of full text, links to various web pages, multimedia files, CDs and other material like statistical data, success stories in rural development, and a data bank on specific topics of current interest. Data on institutions, on-going research programmes, and experts was gathered apart from creating a virtual library with Internet resources (Raju, 2001). The CLIC has now become a central strategic database useful for the faculty and participants of the training programme of NIRD besides the upcountry researchers and other development community members in the country and elsewhere.

Against the outreach programme, a facility called 'Public Information Kiosk (PIK)' was created in the year 2000 at two places viz., Vikarabad and Tenali Public Libraries in cooperation with the Directorate of Public Libraries of Andhra Pradesh Government. PIKs are basically designed as Information-cum-communication facilities not only to create awareness about ongoing rural development programmes with other value added information but also to provide communication tools (Raju, 2000). One Pentium-III computer, scanner, printer, fax and a photocopying machine were installed with Internet connectivity. Locally relevant information on agriculture, health, education, employment and other socio-economic information was gathered, repackaged, supplemented with information from the Internet and displayed in the local language, Telugu. Those that visit the public libraries were initially invited to make use of the facility.

They were also provided with training in sending and receiving e-mails in their local language as well as searching the Internet. Later, as the information was found to be interesting and Internet fascinating though it is English-centric, the visits to the PIKs became fairly regular either to surf the Internet, or to obtain information on employment or who-is-who locally, or to make a photocopy or send a fax. Slowly in two years, the PIKs have become a new dimension of the public libraries. The management of PIKs was later handed over to the Public Library Authority, which has been gladly taken over.

Details about the above two innovations can be seen at the NIRD website www.nird.org.

INFORMATION SEARCHING IN THE INTERNET

With the advent of the Internet the entire scenario of information seeking and information searching has undergone a sea change. Searching the Internet as an important source for information has become common for users as well as librarians of the developing countries who are fortunate to have the connectivity. NIRD being an institution of national importance with the main facts on rural development, its web site (www.nird.org) is being maintained by CORD. Continuous education and training of users about the Internet has become essential to minimize obsolescence. Librarians themselves became resource persons in view of their traditional training and orientation in search techniques (Flecher, 2001). As a result the expression "the interpretation of Internet is librarianship" has gained increasing acceptance.

COMMUNICATION IS THE KEY

To further supplement the range of skills and abilities of the librarian, it is recognized that he should be a good communicator. His ability to articulate effectively the goals and the achievements of the library, the needs of the users, the aspirations of the library staff and the expectations of the top management and external agencies and organizations will play a major role in establishing him as a successful manager. He must be able to present the case of his library, its achievements, and other plus points persuasively in each environment to serve the interests of the library better. Programmes such as LURE will help in that direction.

STRATEGIES FOR ADOPTION

In view of the changing circumstances in the perception of the users, administrators and co-workers, and the impact of new technologies and other environmental changes, the strategies that are to be adopted for a successful organization of the library perhaps may be summarized in the following manner.

1. Change the mind-set of the librarian from a controlling mode of the resources to that of a user satisfaction mode or service mode.
2. Change the librarian from a book-pusher to an 'Information gate-keeper,' with a winning edge.
3. Create a technology infrastructure for participation in networking and delivering repackaged services.
4. Move from 'Just in Case' to 'Just in Time' in an approach to meet the information needs of users.
5. Improve the interpersonal communication skills of the professionals to become more service oriented and dynamic, promote teamwork, and perform effectively.
6. Promote the authentic identity of the library as one of the windows to the human knowledge.
7. Empower cross-functional teams to build expertise across departments to meet overlapping requirements.
8. Uphold traditional library values like free access to knowledge and service to users.
9. Market the library products by developing social marketing skills.

CONCLUSION

In modern times, it is an accepted fact that readers come to the library only to supplement their existing knowledge, as there are other channels of information available to them. In other words, when the other channels fail to satisfy their information needs they may come to the library irrespective of their being rural or urban. Also, to supplement the efforts of users, the librarians should look for opportunities to take the library to the reader as in the case of PIKs. This necessity determines the kind of services that are planned or should be planned to enhance usage of the library. All said and done, in this age of technology, library users are getting familiar with computerized databases, interactive CDs, Internet, e-mail services, and desktop links to a web environment that offers direct access to online databases, full text articles and instant access to electronic journals (Cullen, 2001). They do not just demand access to technology but appear to be accepting it as a fact of life. They seem to know more about what is technologically feasible than the librarian does. Ten years ago this was not the case. Meeting such demands is the challenge the librarian faces today. For a library, though a document oriented information channel, its effectiveness is dependent on the type of documents acquired, and how they are indexed, organized and retrieved expeditiously using information technologies. However, the bottom line is, as a result of our experience with LURE, that the users will keep coming and tapping the door of the library, perhaps if the library has, besides relevant documents, an inviting environment, simple procedures to follow, courteous and knowledgeable staff upholding the traditional values, whether computerized or not. As stated by Lowry (1991), the great libraries of the future will not be those with great collections but those with efficient staff. It is all the more relevant in the digital era.

REFERENCES

Cullen, R (2001): Perspectives on user satisfaction surveys. *Library Trends*, 49(4), 662-686p.

Dayao, Dinna Louise C (1993) : Managers tool box: 100 great management ideas. *World Executive Digest*, February, 1993, 10-15p.

Flecher, PD (2001): Libraries and the Internet: new roles for librarians in a networked world. *Electronic Library*, 19(1), 5-6p.

Lowry, CB (1991): Information technologies and transformation of libraries and librarianship: A changing world. New York, Howarth, 450p.

National Institute of Rural Development (1998): Lure III, a workshop report. (Mimeo)

Raju, KA (1991): Issue paper for the workshop on LURE, Hyderabad, September 30, 1991, National Institute of Rural Development, 8p.

Raju, K.A. (2000) : Towards access to information in rural India. *Information Services and Use*, 20, 27-31p.

Raju, K.A. (2002) : Creation of virtual library for rural development: A case of CLIC. Information Today and Tomorrow, 21(1), 15-16p.

Sebaratnam, JS (1995): Transforming libraries to support change and growth: Meeting the challenges of the 21st Century *in* Networking as the future of libraries: Managing intellectual record an international conference, 19-21, April, 1995, London, University of Bath.

Vavrek, Bernard (1995): Rural information needs and the role of public library, *Library Trends*, 44(1), 21-48p.

Wormell, Irene (1997): The new information professional in library and information science: Parameters and perspectives. Vol. 1, New Delhi, Concept Publications, 53-59p.

How Can the College Libraries of Western China Conform to Digital Trends?

Wang Fang

SUMMARY. There exist many difficulties for the college libraries of western China to develop digital libraries. These difficulties are shortage of funds, restriction of information infrastructure, library leadership, shortage of technical knowledge and user training. After analysis of these problems, this paper sums up some experiences and lessons learned. Based on this, some suggestions on how to solve those problems are put forward, including trying to extend funding sources, improving management knowledge, extending external communication, etc. The conclusion is that in order to provide good information service, the college libraries of western China must make every effort to conform to digital trends. *[Article copies available for a fee from The Haworth Document Delivery Service: 1-800-HAWORTH. E-mail address: <docdelivery@haworthpress.com> Website: <http://www.Haworth Press.com> © 2002 by The Haworth Press, Inc. All rights reserved.]*

KEYWORDS. Western China, digital library, college library, mixed library, China library

Wang Fang is a PhD Candidate, Department of Information Management, Beijing University and Associated Professor at Ningxia University, China (E-mail: ecofan@ccermail.net or wfsusan@ccermail.net).

[Haworth co-indexing entry note]: "How Can the College Libraries of Western China Conform to Digital Trends?" Fang, Wang. Co-published simultaneously in *Science & Technology Libraries* (The Haworth Information Press, an imprint of The Haworth Press, Inc.) Vol. 23, No. 2/3, 2002, pp. 67-75; and: *Leadership and Management Principles in Libraries in Developing Countries* (ed: Wei Wei, Sue O'Neill Johnson, and Sylvia E. A. Piggott) The Haworth Information Press, an imprint of The Haworth Press, Inc., 2002, pp. 67-75. Single or multiple copies of this article are available for a fee from The Haworth Document Delivery Service [1-800-HAWORTH, 9:00 a.m. - 5:00 p.m. (EST). E-mail address: docdelivery@haworthpress.com].

Digital Object Identifier: 10.1300/J122v23n02_08

INTRODUCTION

The western region of China is less developed than the eastern region, including economy, society and culture. Influenced by the external environment, the college libraries of the western region have developed slowly these years, especially in digital construction. On the other hand, the Internet is bringing a new development trend, and the digital library is developing all over the world. This places great pressure on the college libraries in western China. This paper will offer an analysis of the difficulties for the western region to develop digital libraries, sum up the experiences and lessons learned, and put forward some suggestions on how to solve those problems.

DIFFICULTIES FOR THE COLLEGE LIBRARIES OF WESTERN CHINA TO DEVELOP DIGITAL LIBRARIES

Shortage of Funds

In western China, the main investor in college libraries is the government. In China, some universities and colleges are under the direct control of National Education Department, others are under the control of local governments, and others are under the control of other central departments. For the first type of colleges, the funding given to their libraries is part of the total funds of the universities or colleges, which are allocated from National Education Department. In western China, most colleges belong to the second type. The funds are mainly from the local governments, part of which will be appropriated to the library. There are also some funds from other channels such as research programs and from the incomes of college-run businesses. Sometimes libraries can get contributions from the community but in general, college libraries of the western region get fewer contributions than those of the eastern region.

This fund shortage has existed for many years, and has been restricting the construction of library collections and information resources. The main reason is the low percentage increase in appropriation from the government can't meet rapidly increasing book prices. Another reason is that the college libraries of the western region cannot obtain abundant contributions from the community. The direct result of this funding shortage is the gradual decrease of newly bought copies and new format materials. This situation is vastly better than that of public libraries where in the west, some public libraries have not bought one new book because of poor funding in quite a few years, and it is difficult for some libraries to pay the wages of librarians.

As modern information technology comes into use all over the world and greatly influences information service, the digital aspects of a library becomes more and more important and necessary. This means that the traditional western college libraries are facing great pressure. Unfortunately, digital library construction needs a great deal of money, an especially difficult hurdle for the libraries of western China to overcome.

The construction of digital library requires money for hardware (computer equipments and network infrastructure), software, digital information resources funds and training expenses. This is a great investment for many college libraries of the western region and from recent statistics we find that digital library construction is actually making progress. The data shows that the central government is paying more and more attention to the country's information access, including the areas of education and libraries. In fact, information access is one of the most important policies of the central government in a five-year development plan.

Restriction of Information Infrastructure

Compared with the eastern region, the information infrastructure of the western region is relatively backward, except in the areas of higher education where the information infrastructure is more advanced than that of other industries. "Prospering the Country by Science and Education" is a fundamental national policy in China, so the Educational Net is one of the four earliest nets. On this base, college libraries can exchange information easily through the Internet and possess digital access. Other infrastructure conditions such as buildings, computers, LAN infrastructure and trained experts in information technology, are still not sufficient for further development. This will make the digital construction a difficult undertaking in the near future.

Library Leadership

The library director's knowledge about the digital library and its importance are very critical factors for a library's digital progress. From personal experience in the western region, it is clear that many library directors know little about the digital library and in fact some don't know how to send e-mail. Lack of knowledge on how to begin and how to manage a digital program often retards the program's progress. In some libraries, the digital program drags on in the development stage and negatively influences normal daily service.

Management of the digital program is a critical problem, but the knowledge shortfall on program management is a quite common phenomenon. Lack of communication with other regions and the traditional working and thought modes of the employees often can't be changed quickly. Due to this, there is a significant loss of knowledgeable professionals in the western region and it is often difficult for a library to get information and management talents to run the digital program. It is clear that although the library is an information exchange center, directors and librarians themselves are often quite closed in their thought modes. This needs to change in order for programs to be effective.

Shortage of Technical Knowledge

In the west, most librarians are short of technical knowledge in information science because of two reasons. One is that many of them have been working in a library for many years and have no college level academic credentials. This means that their knowledge is becoming outdated. They have learned on the job and without newly educated professionals in the system it is not easy for them to learn about the digital aspects of information. The second leads from the first and lies in the shortage of professional training or education in librarianship. The digital library is a new concept for many librarians in the west and because there aren't departments of library science or information management in many colleges, there is no mechanism for continuing education of librarians even if the library desires it. Vendors are often ready to provide training for the library, but they target only potential customers and provide training on their systems rather than education about the issues.

The shortage of librarians' technical knowledge is sure to hinder the digital process of a library. Some traditional posts will disappear and some entrenched librarians will take various measures to keep their posts and are an obstruction to digital reformation. In order to be effective the construction of a digital library should be similar to the implementation of enterprise resource planning (ERP) because it is not only a technical innovating process, but also a management reforming process. In order to implement the program smoothly, the library also needs to manage the process using Business Process Reengineering (BPR).

User Training

User training is another important factor for a successful digital library program. In western China, the users' information awareness skills need improvement. The information skills referred to include defining information need, understanding information's importance, information retrieval skills, and the knowledge of how to use the Internet and digital library to meet those needs. Certainly, in college libraries, the users have relatively high information awareness. Many professors and researchers have grasped the concepts of how to obtain academic information and are good at using the Internet. But some materials or data are difficult to get from the Internet and so a collection rich digital library system is necessary for those scholars and experts.

LESSONS LEARNED AND EXPERIENCES

Digital progress is not a static equilibrium, but a moving process. Every library has its own lessons and experiences in this area and with regard to the western China college libraries they can be summed up as follows. These lessons were learned over a seven-year tenure in a library in a western China province.

Lessons Learned

Chasing Hi-Tech Blindly

Blindly chasing hi-tech will waste money and time and won't get good results. The digital library offers improved efficiency in the quality of information services, but it is not yet a mature product. In fact, there are few "pure digital libraries" and most libraries are "mixed libraries." There are now many kinds of digital library software on the market but hi-tech plans need a good foundation that is not in place in many libraries. For example, some managers don't know how to choose a database system that fits the specific condition of their libraries. They are often beguiled into thinking that the higher priced or larger systems are better and so make poor choices and a middle-sized library wrongly adopts a system which is suited to a large-sized one.

Overlooking Improving Management Quality

The digital library is not only a technical process, but also a management reforming process that requires BPR. Due to a lack of scientific working process design, assessment, library culture, and an incentive mechanism for employees a library's digital construction often meets with obstructions. The management of a library is not the same as that of an enterprise, but is similar enough to capitalize on the positive aspects of BPR. In digital process, high management quality is a key condition. Many libraries think of digital process only as a technical process. This is a lesson worth learning.

Overlooking Librarian-Training

There is a phenomenon worth special attention in western China libraries. Librarians are often divided into two factions: one is traditional and another is modern. The modern librarians often work with computers, networks and electronic resources and actively seek out digital works. The traditional departments stick with paper documents. This distinction is not an unusual thing, but in many libraries the two parts are differentiated so clearly that the traditionalists know little about what the modernists are doing. They have nothing to do with the digital library construction, in either practice or theory. That this is allowed to happen is a mistake of library administration. The digital library is a modernizing process influencing the entire organization and every librarian should be involved. Only when all the librarians recognize the importance of and most of them grasp the knowledge about its implementation, use, and basic operation, can the digital library program obtain success.

Overlooking User-Training

Not overlooking user training is another lesson worth learning. In western colleges, most teachers, researchers and students know about information retrieval skills, but some are not aware of the Internet or common digital information retrieval methods, especially those aged users. It is necessary for the library to hold training classes regularly to introduce new databases, teach information retrieval methods and increase awareness of both digital and paper documents and their usage. At the same time, by communicating with the users regularly and getting feedback in time, the library can become clear on what users need and make good decisions on the presentation of paper and electronic documents.

Actual Experiences

Combine the Construction of Digital Library with Local Development

With the fund shortage, a good way for the western college libraries to justify increases is by combining the construction of a digital library with local development. Many local colleges offer courses that are related closely to local economic development. The Ningxia Hui Autonomous Region, for example, has many research programs and main tasks are on how best to make use of local economic, social and cultural resources to develop the local economy. So the library of Ningxia University pays lots of attention to the documents and databases on any related programs and subjects. SDI is a useful and important service for them and it is handled more efficiently in a digital library environment.

Correctly Recognize the Significance of "Mixed Library"

"Mixed library" means a middle state between the traditional paper document library and the overall digital library. From the above analysis, we find that there are still many restrictions to hinder the realization of an overall digital library in the western region. The library needs to reinforce the system of traditional document resources while making full use of present conditions to digitalize critical documents, purchase suitable software, to transmit documents digitally, and strengthen inter-library services and sharing of the electronic information resources. It is certain that the "mixed library" is a transitional period that will exist for quite a long time, not only in western libraries, but also in the libraries all over the world.

Communications with Other Libraries and Regions

In the west, there still exist closed ideas about open communication both inside and outside of the library community. Some libraries are either unwilling or simply unable to communicate with other libraries. Some of them are inactive in taking part in academic associations, conferences or academic activities. This means that they might lose some opportunities to know the new trends in digital library development. In order to conform to the developing trend, western Chinese libraries should grasp any possible opportunities and actively create opportunities for young professionals to communicate with the eastern and international libraries and relevant academic associations. Communication can serve a dual purpose by bringing useful information into the area, and by training professionals to form a strong resource backbone for the digital program.

SUGGESTIONS FOR SOLVING THE PROBLEMS

How should the western China academic libraries conform to digital trends? Some suggestions are given below.

Try to Extend Funding Sources

One of the main tasks of a library director is to make every effort to increase the sources of funds. Money is essential to any business and especially to digital library construction. Besides trying to obtain enough money from the government, the director should also be active in building relationships with various enterprises and looking for every opportunity to get contributions form the community.

Improve Management Knowledge

Efficient management guarantees the smooth implementation of a digital library program. Effective process management is necessary to develop a digital program and shouldn't be neglected. It should be taken into careful consideration before the program is implemented. By improving the management processes, the library's working process gets reengineered, the librarians get technical training, and the ideas of the directors become enhanced. All of these are necessary and important to a digital library program.

Import Special Talents

The importance of talent is well known in today's China, but it is quite difficult for the western region to recruit talented individuals and in recent years the brain drain on the region is significant as a great deal of technicians and other qualified personnel have flowed into the east. Many librarians with special expertise also leave the library. This makes it difficult for the library to get further development. As a preparation for the digital program, the library should select some librarians with potential and train them to learn from the successful experiences of other libraries and to grasp technical and management knowledge. In fact, in the west, there are often few librarians who possess the ability for further training because of their poor knowledge base. Therefore, it is a valuable suggestion for the library to import special talent to be in charge of the digital program. The imported expert should also take the responsibility of training the librarians and can decide to stay or leave after accomplishing the program. Flexible forms of utilizing talents are quite important for digital library programs, as well as for the development of western China.

Extend External Communication

Innovation leads to progress and development, but it never comes from closed thought. Innovation needs the renewal of people's thoughts, and this comes from continuous studying and frequent communication. The digital library is a technical and management innovation for a library. In order to realize it, librarians and related leaders of the college need to keep up with the newest knowledge and information. By its nature, the digital library is an open system and communication is an essential characteristic. Communication is particularly important for a college library because of its special academic functions. But in western China, many libraries do not have enough ability to provide opportunities for librarians to take part in various conferences. This combined with lower wages also contributes to the brain drain flowing to the east.

CONCLUSION

"Developing the Western Region" is a fundamental national policy for the country. Two key elements for a region's development are science and education and these are both dependent on access to quality information. The library plays an integral part in the development of western universities and colleges. In order to provide good service, libraries must positively conform to digital library trends. In order to create the optimal conditions for this, western China libraries need to sum up experiences and lessons, and manage effectively to solve the problems outlined in this paper.

Development of a Web Site
for a Commercial Bank Corporate Library
in Sri Lanka

Shivanthi Weerasinghe

SUMMARY. This paper describes the creation, development, and implementation of a corporate library Web site. It gives details of how the author was motivated to deliver Web-based services to the users of the library as a provision of improved services. A brief introduction of the library and its existing services are given. The leadership and management practices that were followed together with problems that were encountered in the process of achieving the objectives are also described. In conclusion, the paper describes lessons learned from the project. *[Article copies available for a fee from The Haworth Document Delivery Service: 1-800-HAWORTH. E-mail address: <docdelivery@haworthpress.com> Website: <http://www.HaworthPress.com> © 2002 by The Haworth Press, Inc. All rights reserved.]*

KEYWORDS. Web-based services, Web pages, library services, planning, leadership, initiative strategies

INTRODUCTION

The Bank of Ceylon Library was established about 25 years ago as a traditional corporate library, and is currently staffed by one professional

---

Shivanthi Weerasinghe is Librarian, Bank of Ceylon, Sri Lanka.

[Haworth co-indexing entry note]: "Development of a Web Site for a Commercial Bank Corporate Library in Sri Lanka." Weerasinghe, Shivanthi. Co-published simultaneously in *Science & Technology Libraries* (The Haworth Information Press, an imprint of The Haworth Press, Inc.) Vol. 23, No. 2/3, 2002, pp. 77-82; and: *Leadership and Management Principles in Libraries in Developing Countries* (ed: Wei Wei, Sue O'Neill Johnson, and Sylvia E. A. Piggott) The Haworth Information Press, an imprint of The Haworth Press, Inc., 2002, pp. 77-82. Single or multiple copies of this article are available for a fee from The Haworth Document Delivery Service [1-800-HAWORTH, 9:00 a.m. - 5:00 p.m. (EST). E-mail address: docdelivery@haworthpress.com].

Digital Object Identifier: 10.1300/J122v23n02_09

librarian and four paraprofessional assistants. Modern library methods and technologies have been introduced over time, with an online library catalog and a computer-based index of periodical titles and holdings, among the notable enhancements.

I joined the organization 14 years ago as the Assistant Librarian. During my tenure, I have continually sought to improve library services by developing more efficient procedures and processes. Upon the retirement of the Head Librarian in 2002 January, I was promoted to that position after six months. Soon after assuming such responsibilities, I introduced an email-based current awareness service that incorporated attachments. This electronic service not only allowed the library to provide a more effective service at less cost, but also enabled it to reassign staff to other library services. The success of this improved current awareness service encouraged me to consider the development and implementation of a Web site for library services. I had previously experimented with the creation of a Web site as the result of training I at received at Training Course on Information Technology for Libraries at the Victoria University of Wellington, New Zealand, that was supported by an IFLA Scholarship.

PLANNING

Vision

As a result this training program, I developed adequate knowledge and skill in the use of HTML and Dream Weaver for creating Web sites. Every lecture in the program emphasized that Librarians, as Information Managers, should be more creative, proactive and innovative in the provision of information services. Such a philosophy inspired me to envision a virtual library for my organization.

Mission

To have the information disseminated through a Library Web site known as the Library and Information Service Web site.

Goal

To complete the Web site by the end of February 2003.

Aspects for Consideration

Before creating and implementing the Web site the following major aspects were thoroughly considered:

1. Why?

As the information needs of decision makers and their support staff increases, it is essential that the corporate library improve and grow in response to such information needs. Existing library and information services were deemed to be inadequate to meet the growing demands of the organization and the time constraints imposed on users. A library Web site offers a cost effective and efficient method of information dissemination and concurrently enhances the visibility and proactive position of the library.

2. For Whom?

The intended Web site was envisioned to serve the information needs of senior management with Internet/Intranet access in the Head Office and the Provincial Offices. As key information gatekeepers, they would subsequently disseminate to their subordinates.

3. What?

The Web site would offer the following types of services:

- new library accessions (e.g., books, periodicals, articles)
- scanned library documents
- Web data and information
- bank related news and information.

Initiative Strategies

As a corporate Web site already existed, it was necessary to demonstrate the need and value of a separate library server and site to the bank's middle and upper management. A proposal was subsequently prepared and submitted to senior management. In the proposal, I outlined the logistics, procedures, and plans associated with the project that included the following:

- connecting through a mail server;
- publicizing and promoting the library Web site;
- purchase of necessary software (e.g., Dream weaver);
- specifications and purchase for other equipment (e.g., scanner); and
- staffing.

The proposal was subsequently approved and I received permission to request support from the organization's Information Technology Department. I was also granted permission to acquire supplemental software and hardware after the Web site was established. In addition, qualified personnel would be reassigned to staff new Web-based services.

Organization

With the approval of the project, I prepared the following implementation schedule:

- complete the Web site plan–31st of December 2002
- complete the designing and creation of the Web site with connections to the intranet–31st of January 2003
- monitor and review the Web site by the Department Head–5th February 2003
- send out the circular and informing through the e-mail–12th February 2003
- launch the Web site–18th February 2003

PLANNING THE WEB SITE

The intended Web site was planned with the library staff members and decided to use the under mentioned Web pages with the main contents. The pages will be linked to the Home Page.

Main/Home Page

Message from the Librarian, mainly to introduce the Web site and partly for marketing overall Library work. Important news alerts.

Library Information Page

New Additions' Index to the Library Collection (books and periodical articles arranged under subject headings) uploaded from the Windows ISIS Program. Annotations of entries.

Internet Information Page

Links to articles and other information searched from the World Wide Web (arranged under subject headings).

Newspaper Information Page

Links to Sri Lanka Newspapers and Newspaper Articles Index (arranged under subject headings).

This plan was submitted to the Head of the Training Department, under which the library functions. It was decided at this stage to include a Web page for the Training Department too with information about overseas training programs and the application forms. This would save the time and paper of printing about 900 application forms.

Training Department Information

Information regarding training programs.

Application form for the training programs.

The design of the Web site was finally completed with the active participation of the team. But it was not completed on the given date.

Assistance from the Information Technology Department to obtain Internet connection was obtained but not without experiencing technical problems since it has been connected through the internal mail server. It was necessary for the IT personnel to check with the main server to clarify that there would not be any effects on the information system of the organization. This actually delayed the final outcome considerably.

The completion of the creation of the Web site was then conveyed to the head of the department for monitoring and reviewing only by the 2nd week of February. It was necessary to monitor and review the ongoing process for attaining the final goal.

Once the Library Web site was ready to be launched, The Assistant General Manager decided to announce it in the forthcoming meeting for their Departmental Corporate Plan. Meanwhile, other internal publicity for the whole project was planned through circular to regarding the "Library and Information Service Web site."

PROBLEMS ENCOUNTERED

The objective of this service was to disseminate information for the users of the Head Office as well as the Province Offices. Yet as the intranet connection was given through the internal mail server it was not possible to be accessed by the province offices. This issue will be discussed with the view of obtaining a separate server connection for the entire institution in information work. However, having a library Web site for the bank during a short period can be considered an successful initiative.

CONCLUSION

What was planned was achieved fulfilling a dream of having our own Web site. I was able to convince the senior management about the importance of a library and information service going to the customer than the customer coming to the library. I also feel that I have achieved it through smooth and careful planning after taking the initiative and the leadership to gain the consent and support of everyone concerned. Furthermore, good communication with the senior management and colleagues made it easy for me to successfully complete the project. Inviting ideas from and working together with the library team helped me to realize the goal of setting up the planned Web site, at least up to this extent, within the planned time frames. I used the above-mentioned processes and involved the members of the organization to work together to advance my plan for the interest of the entire organization. It was a challenge to work within time limits. I feel that if someone is fully aware of what has to be done, is confident, and applies the skills and leadership to implement a job that would definitely turn out to be successful.

I also learned some lessons during the implementation of my project. One of the lessons learned was that one needed to get the connection to the server on time. It is not advisable to wait until all the operational work is completed to attend to other necessary work connected to a project.

Indonesian Libraries in Agriculture and Tropical Biology: Crises, Reforms and the Ongoing Need for International Support

Widharto

SUMMARY. This article reviews the current state of agricultural and tropical biology libraries in Indonesia in light of chronic financial constraints and more recent and adverse changes in government policy. The necessity of both greater internal networking and increased foreign aid is emphasized. *[Article copies available for a fee from The Haworth Document Delivery Service: 1-800-HAWORTH. E-mail address: <docdelivery@haworthpress. com> Website: <http://www.HaworthPress.com> © 2002 by The Haworth Press, Inc. All rights reserved.]*

KEYWORDS. Agricultural libraries, special libraries in tropical biology, Indonesia–libraries, library associations–international aid

INTRODUCTION

Indonesia comprises 17,000 islands stretching across some 3,200 miles along the equator between the Indian and Pacific Oceans, sandwiched between the continents of Asia and Australia. A country

Widharto is Chief Librarian, Seameo Biotrop, Jl. Raya Tajur Km6, P.O. Box 116, Bogor 16001, Indonesia.

[Haworth co-indexing entry note]: "Indonesian Libraries in Agriculture and Tropical Biology: Crises, Reforms and the Ongoing Need for International Support." Widharto. Co-published simultaneously in *Science & Technology Libraries* (The Haworth Information Press, an imprint of The Haworth Press, Inc.) Vol. 23, No. 2/3, 2002, pp. 83-92; and: *Leadership and Management Principles in Libraries in Developing Countries* (ed: Wei Wei, Sue O'Neill Johnson, and Sylvia E. A. Piggott) The Haworth Information Press, an imprint of The Haworth Press, Inc., 2002, pp. 83-92. Single or multiple copies of this article are available for a fee from The Haworth Document Delivery Service [1-800-HAWORTH, 9:00 a.m. - 5:00 p.m. (EST). E-mail address: docdelivery@haworthpress.com].

Digital Object Identifier: 10.1300/J122v23n02_10

rich in natural resources, Indonesia's population stood at more than 209 million people in 2000 with more than 50% inhabiting the island of Java and the remainder distributed over Sumatra, Kalimantan, Sulawesi, Irian Jaya and other islands.

As an increasing population places unprecedented pressure on food supply in Indonesia, debates intensify about ways in which this need can be met in the coming decades. Some argue that agro-chemicals, bio-technology, and modern technology will provide solutions that are reasonably sympathetic to the special biology of tropical systems. For this reason, the capacity of Indonesia to access, generate, disseminate, and promote the utilization of information in the fields of agriculture and tropical biology to be better developed. Both universities and independent research institutions in Indonesia are charged with managing information in these topics, in both print and electronic media. However, the economic crisis affecting Indonesia has had a major adverse impact upon institutional budgets, particularly those for library development in current information sources in science and technology. No library in Indonesia can meet provide a complete array of agricultural or tropical biology sources and stay within budget. This has encouraged many formerly isolated libraries and information services to seek to collaborate in providing coverage, in part by having individual libraries specialize in the particular types of information most appropriate to that institution's strength. But even this is not enough to meet all of Indonesia's needs. Challenges in accessing funding support and expertise from foreign institutions, international relief agencies and library associations will be discussed in this article.

THE INDONESIAN EDUCATIONAL SYSTEM

Education will be instrumental in ensuring that Indonesia competes successfully in AFTA (the Asian Free Trade Association) and in other tough free market arenas. The Indonesian educational system was under Dutch control for about 350 years, followed by the Japanese for 3 years, before it finally proclaimed its status as an independent country named Indonesia in 1945. The statistics of 2000 show that by the end of the 1999 census, there were 150,612 primary schools, enrolling 25,614,836 pupils; 20,866 general junior secondary schools, with 7,600,093 students; 12,069 senior general and vocational schools with 4,778,925 students. There are two types of institutions for higher education, academies and universities. Together they total 1,633 schools, enrolling about three million students.

Purwadi (2000), in his report, stated that the mission of higher education in Indonesia is two fold. First, it prepares students as individuals to learn, apply, develop, and enrich science, technology, and the arts. Second, it prepares them to disseminate those subjects to others to improve economic prosperity and enrich national culture.

THE AGRICULTURAL UNIVERSITY IN INDONESIA

Hoffman (1995), in his report, mentioned that the agricultural colleges and universities in Indonesia are relatively young as professional schools of higher learning. Some have been well funded by the government and/or by bilateral or international funding agencies like USAID (the United States Agency for International Development), JICA (Japan International Cooperation Agency), the ADB (Asian Development Bank) and the WB (World Bank). But many were vocational or diploma schools for decades before they attained professional status. Most have no more than 25 years experience at a genuinely professional level as young institutions; many leave much to be desired in terms of faculty development, laboratory facilities, and libraries. Quite often, funds for maintenance and operating expenses are inadequate.

The agricultural curriculum in many tertiary institutions tends to be heavy on theory and deficient in the practical aspects of farming. This situation prevails wherever the institution does not have adequate farmland or access to commercial farms whether of poultry, livestock, or orchards where students can gain hands-on farming and agribusiness experience.

Ironically, many agricultural colleges and universities have offered masters and doctoral degree programs too soon, before achieving adequate institutional maturity. In many cases, the professors collectively lack serious research experience, and the laboratory and library facilities are only good for the undergraduate level of instruction. The graduate programs compete with undergraduate programs, inevitably resulting in the weakening of the former.

OVERALL LIBRARY DEVELOPMENT IN INDONESIA

An analysis of the existing documentation revealed that Indonesian library systems, be they public, special and university libraries have made relatively slow or no significant progress in a number of key areas (acquisition, budget allocation, membership, and staff strength) in the last decade. Moedjono (1993) stated that the Indonesian libraries as a whole are rated at the lowest level among ASEAN (Association of South East Asian Nations) countries, especially Indonesia's university libraries. Only in the last decade has the library profession begun to receive much attention from the Indonesian government. Although some funding support from various sources are available to these libraries each year, substantially more is required to fully satisfy the national need for an adequate information network. Book and journal prices have risen far higher than the general inflation rate, at the same time as a large increase in the number of new publications (especially journals) has occurred. Additionally, Indonesian rules governing international mail, and banking regulations, particularly currency exchange rates, have hampered the flow of worldwide scientific information into Indonesia, especially foreign journal subscriptions intended for university communities. The combined result of under-funding and bureaucratic over-regulating result has been a deterioration of collections at university libraries. To make matters worse, it has been recently decided that many academic institutions and their libraries will no longer receive any funding from the national government, but rather be put at the financial mercy and unknown attention span of regional government officials, an uncertain prospect in already difficult times.

THE CHALLENGE OF INDONESIAN
AGRICULTURAL LIBRARIES

Not withstanding such obstacles, the Indonesian libraries and librarians must prepare for the information globalization era. Libraries should be skilled enough to handle the more sophisticated tasks of information retrieval, analysis and dissemination, and be ready to adopt new technologies. If the librarians are not themselves ready, library users may not be able to maximize the use of the vast array of technologies that access digital information efficiently. Librarians should be trained and capable of acting as mediators between users and the technologies to retrieve information their clientele request.

Without a sufficiently modern information infrastructure, academic agricultural research and development efforts in developing countries like Indonesia will remain ineffective, for without a means for communicating its results to the productive private sector, academic research ends up having little impact on the economy. Developing countries particularly need information about new foods, animal feeds, and lumber and fiber crops, as well as on food processing, storage, and preservation. Increasingly, fermentation technology and others use microbial processes in the production of foods, beverages, condiments, animal feeds, and medicines are required. Harnessing non-conventional and renewable energy sources, along with utilization of organic wastes, for fuel or for new building materials, while sustaining sufficient potable water supply, have also been added to information needs. Ideally, the library will play an important role in imparting knowledge through acquisition, abstraction, dissemination and promoting awareness of the relevant, up-to-date, productive, and appropriate scientific and technological information acquired through transfer or gained through research.

AN IMPORTANT INTERNATIONALLY FUNDED STUDY ON THE USE OF LIBRARIES FOR AGRICULTURAL RESEARCH

In order to identify the information needs, and any problems related to the use of libraries by agriculturalists at Indonesian research centers and universities attached under the ADB Project INO-1253, an assessment was carried out from February-April 2000. The study, *Increasing access to scientific and technical information on tropical biology for users at SEAMEO-BIOTROP and other institutions during and after economic crisis,* was conducted by the author, with generous support from the ASIA Fellow Program (AFP). The ASIA Fellow Program is the new program funded by the Ford Foundation. It is administered by the International Institute of Education (IIE), in cooperation with the Council of International Exchange Scholars (CIES).

The study included staff users with three different levels of education, S(strata)3 (Ph.D./Doctoral degree), S(strata)2 (Master's degree) and S(strata)1 (Bachelor's degree). Virtually all staff members at the universities make use of their libraries to a significant extent, because they are virtually the only source available for their information needs. Overall, they have a positive attitude toward the library although they recognize that some library resources and services are inadequate. On the question of "User satisfaction with information they obtained," respondents understandably reported quite different levels of satisfaction. Those with terminal S_3 degrees (doctoral/PhD holders) had a much better understanding and expectation of what a good library must be like, and what it must provide to meet their requirements to conduct good research and supplement lecture content. For them, a library that does not subscribe to research journals and provides only textbooks that are out-of date was totally worthless. (Unfortunately, for those seeking a mandate for aggressive upgrading, the S_3 group consisted only of 10 persons.) Those with terminal S1 degrees (BS holders) did not understand what scholarly research is all about, and had difficulty in their assessment of what information is, or is not important. They seemed easily pleased. Those with terminal S_2 degrees (MS holders) fell in between these two groups and their responses may or may not establish the norm of what good library should be.

Ultimately, user responses, comments, problems, and suggestions imply that there were specific areas in which they find the library resources, services and facilities to be particularly inadequate and unsatisfactory. (There were also some services which were not widely known to the respondents and therefore that provided little comment.) Some problem areas identified were: (1) library collections and facilities; (2) language problems; (3) document delivery; (4) application of information technology; and (5) personnel.

Based on this study, the development of an interlibrary loan network among the target universities received the highest priority as a corrective action. Interlibrary loans can be started immediately, at least on a small scale.

SEAMEO-BIOTROP AS AN ALLY OF UNIVERSITY AGRICULTURAL LIBRARIES

SEAMEO (The Southeast Asian Ministers of Education Organization) is an organization created for the purpose of promoting cooperation among Southeast Asian nations through activities in education, science and culture. The organization operates through its 13 Regional Centres located in the member's countries. The SEAMEO, Indonesia, where Regional Centre for Tropical Biology (BIOTROP) is located in Bogor, Indonesia, is where a number of local and some international Agricultural Research Centers are also situated. BIOTROP has been developed to provide the SEAMEO member countries with increased capability in biological sciences relevant to regional economic needs. BIOTROP is internationally supported, and contributes to the economic development of the Southeast Asian region by identifying and solving critical tropical biological problems, through appropriately designed research and training programs.

BIOTROP's Information Resource Unit, to which the library is attached, has not only played an important role in providing information on its subject interests to BIOTROP staff but also to users from elsewhere in Indonesia and from other Southeast Asian countries. Its public service functions include traditional print reference, and access to locally mounted media and electronic sources. In the last two years the BIOTROP library has been connected to the Internet and web-mounted databases. Not surprisingly, through its Higher Education Project (HEP), Indonesia's national Ministry of Education and Culture has formally designated BIOTROP as a major resource center for Indonesian agricultural universities to promote scholarly research via networking.

Over the last few years, the library of BIOTROP has become a partner of the University of Indonesia in organizing training courses on library management and library staffing for the junior librarians from other university libraries in Indonesia. Since 1994, up to six library management and library staff training courses had been carried out. Library management covering strategic planning, total quality management, information technology, human resource management, and marketing of information were topics covered in the courses.

INTERNATIONAL AGENCIES AIDING IN INDONESIAN LIBRARY DEVELOPMENT

Foreign financial assistance, cultural exchanges and international research collaborations have made a profound impact on Indonesian scientific development, including their libraries. The following represent some notable examples.

INTERNATIONAL DEVELOPMENT RESEARCH CENTER (IDRC)

McConnell (1990), in his report, mentioned that since its creation in 1970, Canada's International Development Research Center (IDRC) has allocated more than Can$ 140 million in support of strengthening information systems, services, and tools for development. It has funded over 500 information projects in ninety-five countries. It is actively involved in software development, and maintains one of the most significant development research libraries in the world.

Under IDRC, BIOTROP established the Southeast Asian Weed Information Center (SEAWIC) in 1985. It is a specialized information center about undesirable plants that grow in this region. SEAWIC has been created to select, screen, analyze, process, store, and disseminate information that can be gathered in Southeast Asia. The BIOTROP library collected specialized literature on weeds and prepared abstracts, indexes, bibliographies, and documents. At the end of the project, SEAWIC had successfully produced an expert system for weed identification and weed management purposes for the plantation crops. SEAWIC also publishes newsletters, prepares texts for particular audiences (students, extension workers, administrators working on weeds and its related fields), and also provides answers to technical questions.

UNESCO SPONSORS A LIBRARY SCHOOL
FOR SOUTHEAST ASIA

International organizations such as the UNESCO, FID, and IFLA, have initiated programs for the professional development of librarians. UNESCO has particularly advocated the establishment of library schools in countries where such facilities were not available. Vallejo (1987) in her report stated that in the Philippines, UNESCO sponsored the ten-month intensive post-graduate training course for science information specialists in Southeast Asia (PGTCSIS/SEA) from 1978-1983. This is an inter-country project with Indonesia, Malaysia, the Philippines, Singapore, and Thailand as the original signatories, with China coming later. Thus far the project has produced 146 graduates from 14 countries in the Asian Pacific. Under such programs, more than ten Indonesian librarians (mostly from government institutions) had completed their Master of Library Science.

A NEED FOR CONTINUING EDUCATION OPPORTUNITIES
IN THE USA FOR INDONESIAN LIBRARIANS

The ALA Office of Library Personnel Resources, along with Special Library Association (SLA), American Society for Information Science (ASIS), and the Association of Research Libraries, and Online computer Library Center (OCLC), have long stressed the need for Continuing Education in addition to the initial formal training in library and information science schools. Those opportunities should continue to be extended to assist visiting Indonesian librarians particularly those dealing with the transfer of modern information technology to Indonesian libraries, so that Indonesian librarians on their return can transfer agricultural and biotropical information for appropriate use in the Indonesian economy. A report by Nelson (1994) stresses that new information technologies such as large computerized bibliographic databases allow for access to resources remote to users by e-mail. This is enhanced by digital object identifier links between databases making provision of bibliographic materials over electronic networks easier. Hopefully these developments will overcome isolation among scholarly communities, facilitate sharing of research information and ideas, help reduce unnecessary duplication, provide critical mass of effort needed to give quick answers to pressing problems, and hasten scientific breakthroughs. As reported by Kartosedono (1991), networks for special libraries have now been established in Indonesia. Information sharing on general science and technology is now being coordinated by PDII-LIPI (the Center for Scientific Documentation and Information-Indonesian Institute of Sciences), in Jakarta, while Pustaka (the Central Library for Agriculture and Biology) in Bogor functions as a base for information sharing in agriculture and tropical biology. Continuing support in the procurement of both hardware and software will be an ongoing requirement for the sustained development of these growing Indonesian library network systems.

DISCUSSION AND CONCLUSIONS

With the shift of the primary development of libraries from central to local government and to local people, each region will urgently need up-to-date information and information services, without having Central Government funds. Given the explosion of new information sources and electronic technologies, and ongoing constraints on financial resources, resource-sharing networking have emerged as an important alternative for coping.

Training and continuing education opportunities for the Indonesian librarians will continue to be heavily dependent on successful networking and marketing among individual libraries and librarians. Funding Agencies, such as Asia Foundation, the ASEAN Foundation, the Ford Foundation, the British Council, and other International Institutions such as SLA (Special Library Association), IFLA (International Federation of Library Association) should be approached for financial support and library materials acquisition. The other research institutions, as well as universities in ASEAN member countries, should be asked for donations/exchanges of published materials in those institutions.

REFERENCES

Hoffman, H.K.F. 1995 "Status of agricultural education and challenges for International agencies." IN: *Education for Agriculture*, Proceedings of the Symposium on Education for Agriculture (pp. 73-85), IRRI (The International Rice Research Institute), Manila, the Philippines, 12-16 Nov. 1994.

Indonesia Biro Pusat Statistik. 2000 *Statistik Indonesia = Statistical Year Book of Indonesia.* Jakarta, Biro Pusat Statistik. 590p.

Kartosedono, Soekarman. 1991. "Library development in Indonesia." In: *New challenges in library services in the developing world.* Proceedings of the Eighth Congress of Southeast Asian Librarians (CONSAL) (pp. 19-27), Jakarta, Indonesia, 11-14 June 1990.

McConnell, Paul. 1990 "Information for development: experiences of the International Development Research Center." In: *Information Development.* The International Journal for librarians, Archivists and Information specialists, 6 (1): 8-19.

Moedjono, Parlinah. 1993 "Service within universities communities." In: *Proceeding the Eighth Congress of Southeast Asian Librarians (CONSAL)* (pp. 107-114), Jakarta, Indonesia, 11-14 June 1990.

Nelson, John and John Farrington. 1994 *"Information exchange networking for agricultural development: a review of concepts and practices."* Exceter, Technical Center for Agricultural and Rural Cooperation (ACP-EEC). 86p.

Purwadi, Agung and Suheru Mulyoatmodjo. 2000 "Education in Indonesia: coping with challenges in the third millennium." *Journal of Southeast Asian Education* 1(1): 79-102.

Vallejo, Rosa M. 1987. "Post professional and research studies: the concept of a regional library school." In *Proceedings of the Seventh Congress of Southeast Asian Librarians (CONSAL)* (pp. 169-175), Manila, the Philippines, 15-21 Feb. 1987.

Widharto. 2000 *"Increasing access to scientific and technical information on tropical biology for users at SEAMEO-BIOTROP and other Institutions during and after the economic crisis in Indonesia,"* final report. Bogor, ASIA Fellow Program. 42p.

Library Services–
Application of Management Principles

Pradnya Yogesh
Alan Dalton

SUMMARY. This paper is about enhancing customer satisfaction in a corporate library. The focus is on providing information through connecting and networking people and managing the environment for collaboration. *[Article copies available for a fee from The Haworth Document Delivery Service: 1-800-HAWORTH. E-mail address: <docdelivery@haworthpress.com> Website: <http://www.HaworthPress.com> © 2002 by The Haworth Press, Inc. All rights reserved.]*

KEYWORDS. Library services, customer satisfaction

INTRODUCTION

Over a 5-year period Mahindra-British Telecom (MBT) Ltd. with 2,600 software professionals spread across six development centers spread across the globe, worked on enhancing its library customer service. The library profile is given in Table 1.

Pradnya Yogesh, MLibISc, BSc, is Librarian, Mahindra-British Telecom Ltd., Pune, India (E-mail: yogeshpr@mahindrabt.com). Alan Dalton is Aeronautical Engineer, Training and Management Consultant and Owner of the firm Alan Associates, Pune, India (E-mail: aland@vsnl.com).

[Haworth co-indexing entry note]: "Library Services–Application of Management Principles." Yogesh, Pradnya, and Alan Dalton. Co-published simultaneously in *Science & Technology Libraries* (The Haworth Information Press, an imprint of The Haworth Press, Inc.) Vol. 23, No. 2/3, 2002, pp. 93-96; and: *Leadership and Management Principles in Libraries in Developing Countries* (ed: Wei Wei, Sue O'Neill Johnson, and Sylvia E. A. Piggott) The Haworth Information Press, an imprint of The Haworth Press, Inc., 2002, pp. 93-96. Single or multiple copies of this article are available for a fee from The Haworth Document Delivery Service [1-800-HAWORTH, 9:00 a.m. - 5:00 p.m. (EST). E-mail address: docdelivery@haworthpress.com].

TABLE 1. MBT Library (1997 and 2003)

Parameters	Oct. 1997	Feb. 2003
Open hours per week	40	64
Library staff	1	3
Book stock	400	3283
Journal titles	75	50
Reader spaces	15	36
Square feet of shelving	350 sq. ft.	600 sq. ft.
Square feet of floor space	500 sq. ft.	2000 sq. ft
Registered users (Pune, only)	175	700
Employees (Pune, only)	400	950
Total Employees (worldwide)	850	2,600
Transactions per day	75	300
IT workspaces (Workstations)	1	7
Budget of the library	Rs. 660,000	Rs. 3,500,000

THE FIRST STEPS

The first step was to introduce Information Technology into the library. A state-of-the-art, fully integrated, web-based library software that included an integrated bar code system was installed. This became the backbone of the library service.

Streamlining of the library processes followed. They included:

- Library resources acquisition
- Cataloging
- Circulation
- Automated advance and overdue reminders
- On-line library-item reservations
- Automated reserved-book collection notices
- Permanent borrowing for projects
- Book selection

NEW INITIATIVES–LIBRARY SERVICE ENHANCEMENTS

Web services through the Intranet further raised the level of service. These included:

- Web-OPAC
- Library web site
- E-books
- E-current contents–books and magazines

The electronic current awareness service (eCAS) kept users updated and eliminated geographical barriers, and was well appreciated across the organization. Electronic selective dissemination of information (eSDI) saved users time, and further improved user satisfaction.

ALIGNING WITH CUSTOMER NEEDS

This was implemented in 3 ways.

Listening to the voice of the customer (VOC): Regular meetings are held with senior members of MBT to understand their needs in line with the overall business initiatives.[1 & 2]

Communication with customers: Periodic surveys and questionnaires are used to obtain information on customer satisfaction levels, and to modify and strengthen the library processes.

Customer feedback: A standard feedback form is available on the library's web site, and these are evaluated at regularly scheduled focused group meetings that can immediately discuss any level of dissatisfaction.

Promoting Library Services

Educating Users

Users and management were educated on possible library support business goals. A project-based document repository and retrieval system under the aegis of the library was initiated.

Building Learning Communities[3,4,5 & 6] (Share-and-Learn Sessions)

Every fortnight, the library organizes in the library sessions of internal or external experts to share their insight, views with others. This brings awareness to library resources and also helps:

- Meet user needs
- Give the expert or that group visibility
- Spread the importance of sharing

- Motivate others to share
- Connect knowledge seekers with knowledge owners

Building Social Capital to Leverage Knowledge Sharing[7]

Periodic exhibitions of artifacts and books helped connect people with similar interests. During these events knowledge is also gained serendipitously.

Creating Virtual Networks

The creation of virtual networks brought like-minded people together. This helps experts to share specific knowledge gained besides providing a forum for tacit knowledge sharing. At present there are 15 networks and over 1,000 subscribers.

CONCLUSION

Finally, achieving and sustaining higher levels of customer satisfaction is a continuous challenge for librarians. The inspiration to grow personally and help develop the MBT library services for higher levels of customer satisfaction came from many of the SLA initiatives.

NOTES

1. Tufloy, Charles, 2002. The key to a librarian's success: Developing entrepreneurial traits. *Information Outlook*, 6(6) : 42-47.
2. Clair, Guy St. and Reich, Martina. Knowledge services: Financial strategies and budgeting. *Information Outlook*, 6(6) : 26-33.
3. Canga, Jeff De, 2000. Exploring common knowledge: An interview with Nancy Dixon. *Information Outlook*. 4(4) : 24-32.
4. Koenig, M. D. E. "Knowledge management, user education and librarianship." Paper presented at 67th IFLA Council and General Conference, Boston, MA, 16-25 August 2001.
5. Davenport, Thomas and Prusak, Laurence. 2000. *Working knowledge: How organizations manage what they know.* Boston : Harvard Business School Press.
6. Lamb, Cheryl, 2001. Creating a collaborative environment: The human element. *Information Outlook* 5(5) : 22-25.
7. Canga, Jeff De, 2001. Keeping good company: A conversation with Larry Prusak. *Information Outlook* 5(5) : 36-43.

SUB SAHARAN AFRICA

The Application of Leadership and Management Principles and Strategies in a Bureaucratic Environment: The Case of Federal Ministry of Industry Headquarters Library, Nigeria

Imo J. Akpan

SUMMARY. Contemporary technologies have transformed the information industry. For the library to meet the challenges of the new trends of information usage and consumptions, librarians need more than proficiency in modern technology usage. Appropriate leadership and management strategies need to be employed in library management. This article examines the leadership qualities and managerial strategies of a seasoned library manager

Imo J. Akpan is Librarian, Federal School of Radiography Medical Compound, Yaba, Lagos–Nigeria (E-mail: richimoh@yahoo.com).

[Haworth co-indexing entry note]: "The Application of Leadership and Management Principles and Strategies in a Bureaucratic Environment: The Case of Federal Ministry of Industry Headquarters Library, Nigeria." Akpan, Imo J. Co-published simultaneously in *Science & Technology Libraries* (The Haworth Information Press, an imprint of The Haworth Press, Inc.) Vol. 23, No. 2/3, 2002, pp. 97-102; and: *Leadership and Management Principles in Libraries in Developing Countries* (ed: Wei Wei, Sue O'Neill Johnson, and Sylvia E. A. Piggott) The Haworth Information Press, an imprint of The Haworth Press, Inc., 2002, pp. 97-102. Single or multiple copies of this article are available for a fee from The Haworth Document Delivery Service [1-800-HAWORTH, 9:00 a.m. - 5:00 p.m. (EST). E-mail address: docdelivery@haworthpress.com].

at the Federal Ministry of Industry in Nigeria. The impact of his work on library personnel and the overall effectiveness of the library are considered. The necessity of strong leadership and managerial expertise in meeting the challenge of the present knowledge age are emphasized. *[Article copies available for a fee from The Haworth Document Delivery Service: 1-800-HAWORTH. E-mail address: <docdelivery@haworthpress.com> Website: <http://www. HaworthPress.com> © 2002 by The Haworth Press, Inc. All rights reserved.]*

KEYWORDS. Bureaucracy, communication, contemporary technologies, deregulation, human resources, information access, information industry, information sources, library management, library service, library objectives, leadership qualities, management strategies, managerial acumen, professional development, technical competence, technological innovation

INTRODUCTION

The need for librarians with strong leadership and managerial qualities in today's global information environment is greater than ever. Contemporary trends in the consumption and use of information pose a challenge to librarians, and many of the basic tenets of library management must consequently be reviewed and refined.

The view of Iloege (2001) is that the degree to which the library will remain the central custodian of information access will depend on the extent to which librarians can apply contemporary technological innovations to library operations and services. Omekwu (2001) emphasized that new skills, strategies, services, information sources, and innovative system use, administration, maintenance and development are essential if professionals are to rise to the challenge of the new knowledge/information age. He further stated that, in response to the challenges facing them, librarians will emerge as educators, information managers, consultants, providers, custodians and change agents.

The success of librarians in rising to these challenges, however, will depend on the quality of their leadership and their managerial expertise. The implementation of new technology can succeed only with effective management.

CHANGING TRENDS IN LIBRARIANSHIP

Global trends are resulting in ongoing change in the management of libraries. Increased efficiency, the streamlining and simplification of operations, liberalisation, and deregulation are among many trends in the current global economy that library managers must embrace in the 21st century. Librarians must therefore acquire and employ both leadership and management expertise that will enable them to respond to this environment. Beside the technical competencies involved in running a library, leadership and managerial acumen and expertise will play a critical role in fulfilling such library missions as meeting library users' information needs and imparting life-long learning skills. No library can achieve its aim of user satisfaction or fulfill its obligations to its users without proper mobilization, organization, control, utilization and maximization of its human resources. Hence the need for effective leadership and management principles and strategies. These involve the aggregate planning, organizing, controlling and coordination of the human component of the library by a visionary, inspiring and exemplary leader capable of building a united team.

According to Ajaja (2003), "good leaders are those who make things happen rather than those who simply administer." A leader determines the fate of the organization. S/he motivates members with a view to achieving greater efficiency and inspiring integrity, deep conviction, enthusiasm, persistence, and warmth. S/he is approachable and realistic. A leader should have the ability to focus team members' attention on a common vision or goal. S/he should be able to motivate team members and communicate a strong sense of purpose in performing the work.

LEADERSHIP OF MR. L. B. OGUNDANA

An excellent case in which library objectives were achieved through effective leadership was observed at the Federal Ministry of Industry headquarters Library. The author worked here as a circulation librarian during the tenure of Mr. L. B. Ogundana as the Head Librarian. This seasoned leader/manager-librarian clearly demonstrated that success can be achieved under difficult circumstances created by organizational bureaucracy and red tape.

CHARACTERISTICS OF THE NIGERIAN CORE PUBLIC SECTOR

The Nigerian Civil Service is characterized by bureaucracy, adherence to precedence and resistance to change. Lack of motivation and lack of accountability are commonplace. Constructive criticism is often not well received. In the past, there has been little success in changing this situation. Over the two years of Mr. L. B. Ogundana's tenure in the Ministry, however, the Library was transformed. Most of the Ministry staff, including those in the higher echelons of the Ministry, like the directors and the Honourable Minister, came to recognize the value of the Library's services. This was clear from appraisals and from the increased use of the library.

This achievement was made possible through the good leadership style and managerial expertise of Mr. L. B. Ogundana which are discussed in the following section.

Distinctive Features of Mr. L. B. Ogundana's Administration

The library plan/program was designed to address deficiencies which have hitherto impeded library operation and services. Steps taken included significant changes in personnel and the acquisition of basic subject textbooks and encyclopedias. The integration of information technology into the library operation and services was of central importance in the year 2001 workplan.

The rigid, monotonous civil service schedule was modified. New staff schedules were designed to take care of present realities in the library. For example, catalogers were actively engaged in activities other than cataloging work, rather than remaining idle, during a period of time that the library was unable to acquire new materials to be cataloged.

Through proper coordination and control of the library team, efficient and effective service was offered to clients. Mr. L. B. Ogundana was able to organize the library staff into an effective team. The library staff worked cooperatively irrespective of rank and status (unusual in the civil service environment). Mr. L. B. Ogundana always emphasized the importance of a family atmosphere among staff.

The vision, goals and objectives of the library were clearly communicated to team members. The focus of the objectives was on the delivery of effective and efficient information service to staff, scholars, industrialists, and researchers from within as well as from outside the ministry.

As a leader he emphasized the development of professional competencies of staff/team members. Professional development was employed as a means of motivating employees. Staff members participated in training sessions and conferences on a rotating basis. Because of these incentives, all staff members performed their work with enthusiasm.

Mr. L. B. Ogundana led by example. He emphasized punctuality, and he sometimes arrived at the office by 6:00 GMT, one hour earlier than the official opening hour of 7:00 GMT and occasionally worked until 17:00 GMT without taking official overtime.

With a view to upgrading the quality of services, Mr. L. B. Ogundana transferred approximately six non-professionals out of the library while new professional librarians were recruited.

Mr. L. B. Ogundana displayed exceptional professional competencies in most of the basic areas of librarianship, including cataloging and classification, information retrieval and professional writing. He was actively involved in library association activities. His tenure as chairman of the Association of Government Libraries witnessed many new, positive developments in government library circles.

His leadership style was inspiring; his interactions with team members were always positive. Proposals were often turned down by directors but he persisted without fail in the pursuit of fulfilling library objectives.

In most instances proposals, file-notes, etc., were used to communicate with superiors in higher management. Staff meetings (open forum), notice boards, circulars and telephone were the major channels of communication with the general staff. For closer team members, namely the professional librarians, verbal communication were sometimes used.

LESSONS LEARNED

Some of the useful lessons derived from working with the team at F.M.I. library are listed. Without a good leader/administrator to steer a library in the right direction, a library will not have a focus. Lack of focus can cause a library to become irrelevant to an organization. Absence of good leadership often results in a failure to meet library objectives. Good leaders can achieve library objectives despite obstacles originating from within the library itself, as well as from elsewhere within the organization at large. Departure from precedent is necessary if meaningful and realistic change is to be achieved. Effective communication can be used to break resistance to innovations.

CONCLUSION

Librarians in developing countries need more than proficiency in the use of contemporary technologies. If technologies and human resources are to play meaningful roles in the current knowledge age, appropriate leadership and managerial skill are essential. Omekwu (2003) maintains that for libraries in developing economies to make a sustainable difference in the knowledge age, librarians need to become involved in the development and use of legislative instruments as well as information and human resources policies in the management of libraries.

REFERENCES

Ajaja, Ariyo A. Leadership qualities in a changing management environment. *The Guardian* Monday 25th Feb. 2003.

Bennis, Warren. *On Becoming a leader.* Perseus press 1994.

Bennis, Warren and Bert Nanus. *Leaders: the strategies for taking charge.* New York: Harper and Row, 1985.

Drucker, P.F. *The effective executive.* New York: Harper Business, 1993.

Harvard Business Review on Leadership. Boston, MA: Harvard Business School Press, 1990.

Omekwu, Charles. *Managing information and technology in the knowledge age: A pacesetting Agenda for libraries and librarian of developing cultures.* (Conference paper, Owerri 2001).

Iloege, M.U. *Libraries and librarians: Making a difference in the knowledge age: Imperative for delivery life-long information across space and time in the E-Age.* (Conference paper, Owerri 2001).

The Role of Mobile Patient Library Services in Providing Palliative Care to People Living with HIV/AIDS in Uganda

Michael Kasusse

SUMMARY. The Mildmay Centre Kampala offers training and palliative care to patients living with HIV/AIDS in Uganda. Within the clinic, there is an information resource centre which serves patients, carers, staff, participants, general public, other statutory and voluntary organisations. The leadership and management principles such as principles for transformation of people, for transformation of change, results driven principles, business acumen principles and principles for establishing coalitions/communication are highlighted in the success of providing palliative care to people living with HIV/AIDS in Uganda using the new Mobile Patient Library Services project. *[Article copies available for a fee from The Haworth Document Delivery Service: 1-800-HAWORTH. E-mail address: <docdelivery@ haworthpress.com> Website: <http://www.HaworthPress.com> © 2002 by The Haworth Press, Inc. All rights reserved.]*

KEYWORDS. Library services, HIV/AIDS, palliative care, leadership, management, principles, Uganda

Michael Kasusse, MSc, is Chief Librarian/Information Scientist, The Mildmay Centre, P.O. Box 24985, Kampala, Uganda (E-mail: lkasussem@yahoo.com).

[Haworth co-indexing entry note]: "The Role of Mobile Patient Library Services in Providing Palliative Care to People Living with HIV/AIDS in Uganda." Kasusse, Michael. Co-published simultaneously in *Science & Technology Libraries* (The Haworth Information Press, an imprint of The Haworth Press, Inc.) Vol. 23, No. 2/3, 2002, pp. 103-112; and: *Leadership and Management Principles in Libraries in Developing Countries* (ed: Wei Wei, Sue O'Neill Johnson, and Sylvia E. A. Piggott) The Haworth Information Press, an imprint of The Haworth Press, Inc., 2002, pp. 103-112. Single or multiple copies of this article are available for a fee from The Haworth Document Delivery Service [1-800-HAWORTH, 9:00 a.m. - 5:00 p.m. (EST). E-mail address: docdelivery@haworthpress.com].

Digital Object Identifier: 10.1300/J122v23n02_13

INTRODUCTION

Observations on the theme are made at The Mildmay Centre, Kampala. The Mildmay centre is a British NGO collaborating with government of Uganda through the ministry of health and is funded by The U.S. Centres for Disease Control and Prevention. It provides comprehensive out patient palliative care and rehabilitative services for men, women and children living with or affected by HIV and AIDS. Holistic (whole person) care is given with an emphasis on quality, professionalism and respect for the rights and beliefs of each individual. The centre aims to remain at the forefront of this speciality and to improve the care of people with AIDS through education and by the demonstration of relevant, culturally sensitive and innovative models of care. It has an out patient clinic, pastoral care services and study centre where participants mostly from the Sub Saharan Africa attend short courses in HIV/AIDS care and treatment. Within the clinics at the centre, there is an Information Resource Centre of which I am the Chief Librarian/Information Scientists.

HIV/AIDS Status in Uganda

The HIV infection rates from the major sentinel surveillance sites continue to show declining trends. The decline continue to be most significant in the young age groups 15-24 years. Likewise data from the AIDS Information centre continues to show declining HIV Sero-prevalence among young persons seeking voluntary counselling and testing. In spite of the observed dent in the HIV/AIDS epidemic, the HIV infection rates are still unacceptably high. There is a need to sustain these achievements and increase to even higher levels of awareness and ensure that they transform into higher levels of behaviour change.

As of 31st December 2001, a cumulative total of 55,861 AIDS cases (children and adults) had been reported to the surveillance units of the STD/AIDS control programme. Of the reported, 92.7% are adults while 7.3 are children aged 12 years and below. Of the adults, 45.9% were males while 54.1% were females. The overall mean age for adults was 32.22 years and 31.32 years for males and females respectively. The above shows the extent to which the youth and women are being hit by the epidemic. Behavioural surveillance is increasingly becoming a major component of the surveillance system for HIV/AIDS in the country especially in light of the declining HIV infection trends. Data from surveys carried out over the last few years shows high levels of knowledge of protection from HIV/AIDS, increase in condom use and condom use in non-regular partnerships, and the sustainability of the increased age at first sex. Many people are now becoming infected with HIV from sex with stable partners. In rural Uganda, cohort married women less than 25 years had the highest HIV sero prevalence (Nunn et al., 1994), indicating a high risk for individuals in stable partnerships. A consistent finding in many parts reveals that condoms are less likely to be used with stable partners. In Uganda, 4% reported condom use with a spouse, 19% with regular partners and 44% with casual partners (McCombie, 1999).

INFORMATION SERVICE OFFERED AND NOT OFFERED AT THE INFORMATION RESOURCE CENTRE (IRC)

The IRC offers health related information to its users who include patients, carers, general public, staff, participants, other statutory and voluntary organisations, self help and support groups, but it doesn't give advice about treatments or other health-related choices. It also offers benefit information, including which benefits are available, and who can help with benefit enquiries (it does not liase with the benefits agency or advice about entitlement) provides information about a range of health services but can't ensure suitability of these services; offers details about self-help and support groups, introduce clients other appropriate agencies and making initial contacts for them but it does not accompany clients to self-help and support groups or guarantee the quality of support offered; by agreement the IRC can offer practical support to new self-help and support groups, e.g., designing leaflets and posters, typing minutes, distributing information advice, etc. It does not offer practical support to groups who receive funding in order to pay for practical support services; it provides information which comes from a legitimate source; it can't guarantee the accuracy or validity of information provided; above all, IRC are proud of the new Mobile Patient Library Service which works hand in hand with Occupation Therapy and Home visit department.

APPLICATION OF LEADERSHIP AND MANAGEMENT PRINCIPLES AT THE IRC

These principles empower one with leadership responsibility for envisioning the future of an information systems and setting goals to achieve that future, choosing and leading the best possible staff, managing resources wisely, fundraising, seeing that exciting new programs get implemented, and assuring that the technology is there to support those programs. The profession of librarianship and libraries themselves are on an evolutionary path, the future destination of which is not wholly clear. According to Martha Kyrillidou and Stanley Wilder, defining where we are now in terms of how we utilise our human resources is useful. By depicting the current situation, we can more vividly see both how far we have come and how far we have yet to go to meet our ideas.

Jennifer James (1997) describes the skills necessary for "thinking in the future tense": perspective, pattern recognition, cultural knowledge (understanding the myths that undergird our daily lives in the workplace and society), flexibility, vision, energy, intelligence, and global values. She emphasises to avoid becoming a "self-sealing culture." It is upon this emphasis that we came up with the new Mobile Patient Library Services. Application of Leadership and Management Principles and Strategies is mainly focussed at the new Mobile Patient Library Services project.

I designed and implemented the new Mobile patient library services project which has now completed one year with the goal of contributing to the palliative care to HIV/AIDS patients in Uganda.

Palliative care is defined by the WHO as the total care of someone who has an incurable progressive illness. The primary aim of total holistic care is not to prolong life but to improve or to maintain quality of life as long as possible, and to ensure that death is achieved with dignity and in comfort and palliative care is ideally provided by an interdisciplinary team working in partnership with the patient, spouse/partner and family. Due to the nature of illness, patients may receive physical health complications where the doctor advises them to stay at home. Others may be admitted temporarily to hospitals waiting to be reviewed by specialists. These patients are visited by the centre team that offers extended palliative care. This library service is an added service to the existing patient home/hospital visits team facilitated by the entire organisation. Initially the patient visit team included a doctor, a nurse, counsellor, occupational therapist and a driver. With this new library service, a librarian/information scientist was added to the team.

Aim/Goal of the Project

The aim of the mobile patient library services is to provide information materials to patients at home or in government hospital beds and their carers.

Objectives of the Project

The specific objectives of the mobile patient library services are to disseminate relevant, timely information to patients and carers that can greatly improve the condition of the patient; increase awareness about HIV/AIDS and treatment; occupy the patient and carers during the time of patients sickness and to make information service be part of the holistic patient care offered during palliative care.

Information Services Offered by the Project

The specific services offered are the provision of books, especially novels; provision of our Newsletter and Journals such as Positive Living; as a carer, involving relatives and friends: a good practice guide for homes for older people, gardening in homes, guilt, etc.; designing simple and easy to understand brochures about nutrition, drug administration, health services, physical therapy, etc.; providing current awareness services especially anti retroviral drugs access and selective dissemination of information to specific patients; provision of talking books service, i.e., where a female or male voice of a person is recorded on cassettes while reading a book, novel, brochure, chat and certain articles of journals. For a client to receive this service he must have a radio cassette. If a patient dies, carers can continue to receive the information service for as long as they meet the requirements. So far there are 35 titles of recorded cassettes. We hope to have more titles this year. Each member is visited once every two weeks. When the member comes to the clinic for other services, an assessment is made when to make a visit. The most significant difficulty addressed by the project is the poor information seeking behaviour among patients hence the need for effective dissemination of health related information to patients and carers.

Membership

There is free membership for the information services offered at the IRC to members mentioned above. Also the home visits are made free to any patient registered with the Mildmay centre and who meets a certain criteria for the home/hospital visit team. However for one to receive the information services offered by the project, one has to be registered with the IRC and the Mildmay Centre and pay an annual registration fee of US $40. At this fee, services are extended to immediate carers if they can come to the Mildmay Centre (IRC) or stay at the home of the patient.

Evaluative Statistics

I will use the simplest form of statistics. These show the number of members that are registered under the project.

Period

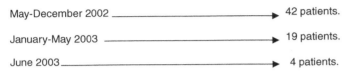

May-December 2002 ⟶ 42 patients.

January-May 2003 ⟶ 19 patients.

June 2003 ⟶ 4 patients.

The total registration of members is 65 patients but 6 patients have passed away and the services are extended to the carers. At the moment this number is high compared to the resources and staff available. This is seriously affecting the effective provision of information services. Also the integration of the library services with those of the home visit team affects the provision of library services such as the following of catchment area of the Home/hospital team in order to become a member. There is need to have a separate program that is fully funded for providing this kind of service.

The leadership and management principles are personal and professional attributes that are critical to successful performance. A leader and a manager of an information system must understand and follow the principles discussed below in order to attain successful performance. I will categorise these principles into 5 groups as follows:

a. Principles for transformation of people.
b. Principles for transformation of change.
c. Results driven principles.
d. Business Acumen principles.
e. Principles for establishing coalitions/communications.

PRINCIPLES FOR TRANSFORMATION OF PEOPLE

These include the principle of integrity/honesty which demonstrates a sense of corporate responsibility and commitment to information service and creates a culture that fosters high standards of ethics; conflict management for managing and resolving conflicts and disagreements in a positive and constructive manner to minimise negative impact; leveraging diversity that leads and manages an inclusive workplace that maximises the talents of each person to achieve sound results by having shared leadership. Respects, understands, values and seeks out individual differences to achieve the vision and mission of the organisation; and the principle of team building which inspires, motivates, and guides others toward goal accomplishments. Develops leadership in others through coaching, mentoring, rewarding, and guiding employees hence developing a common mission.

In this project we used the principle of leveraging by having shared leadership. Shared leadership where the organisation places a higher degree of importance on the roles people assume than on the positions they hold. For example, whereas my position may tell me that I manage the circulation department, my role tells me that I am there to make sure that users are satisfied. Moving into shared leadership means adopting different views of individual roles and systems especially training and coaching systems. We have seen training as an important element in preparing staff to take on new roles. It is especially important for the development of managers who often have exerted leadership through the authority of their positions.

According to Katzenbach (1998), developing a common mission may seem like a simple task, but it is not. Following the leadership principle of team building, we were successful in our new services because we were willing to shape a common mission outside the unit-specific mission, interested in sharing jargon and definitions of technical terms, willing to learn aspects of the other partners' expertise and able to appreciate differences and not criticising others' professions.

PRINCIPLES FOR TRANSFORMATION OF CHANGE

These principles include flexibility which is to adapt behaviour and work methods in response to new information, changing conditions, or unexpected obstacles; principle of resilience that is to recover quickly from setbacks and effectively balance personal life and work; external awareness which is to identify and keep up to date on key national and international information policies that affect information work; creativity and innovation which develops new insights into situations and applies innovative solutions towards improvement of information work and satisfying user needs; service motivation that creates and sustains an organisational culture which encourages others to provide the quality of service essential to high performance of information work; continual learning principle that is to recognise own strengths and weaknesses and to seek feedback from others and opportunities to master new knowledge; strategic thinking which examines information policy issues and strategic planning with a long-term perspective and to determine objectives and sets priorities, anticipates potential threats or opportunities and principle of vision for long-term views and acts as a catalyst for organisational change, builds a shared vision with others. Influences others to translate vision into action.

Following the principle of creativity and innovation, the librarian remains informed about changes in how library users use the library and what users need in terms of information services. S/he should be aware of developments in other libraries and in the library profession. With this we designed and implemented The Mobile Patient Library Services with the aim of reaching out clients who can't come to the library because of sickness. Also following the principle of strategic thinking, I am a member of a number of committees and task force for the entire Mildmay Centre, e.g., member of the planning committee of Mildmay International Support Clients Association. This helps to develop policies on information issues but also serve the larger community in tasks that may have little or no direct bearing on the library or on information work.

RESULTS DRIVEN PRINCIPLES

These include entrepreneurship which is to identify opportunities to develop and market new information products and services within or outside of the organisation; principle of decisiveness which is proactive and achievement oriented: it is to exercise good judgement by making sound and well-informed decisions, perceive the impact and implications of decisions, make effective and timely decisions, even when data is limited or solutions produce unpleasant consequences; technical credibility which is to understand linkages between administrative competencies and mission needs for information work; principle of customer service that provides for balancing interests of a variety of clients, readily readjusts priorities to respond to pressing and changing client demands, anticipates and meets the information need of clients, achieves quality end-products, is committed to continuous improvement of information services; and accountability which assures that effective controls are developed and maintained to ensure the integrity of the organisation. Holds self and others accountable for rules and responsibilities.

BUSINESS ACUMEN PRINCIPLES

These include a financial management principle that demonstrates a broad understanding of principles of financial management and marketing expertise necessary to ensure appropriate funding levels, monitors expenditures in support of programs and policies and identifies cost-effective approaches; human resources management principle for assessing current and future staffing needs based on organisational goals and budget realities, using merit principles, ensures staff are appropriately selected, developed, utilised, appraised, and rewarded, takes corrective action; and a technology management principle that provides for efficient and cost-effective approaches to integrate technology into the workplace and improve program effectiveness, develops strategies using new technology to enhance decision making, understands the impact of technological changes on the organisation.

Following the principle of financial management, a librarian negotiates with organisations and individuals outside the library to secure funding, reach agreements on key issues, and safeguard the interests of the library. Also to lead effort to identify needs that cannot be adequately supported by the parent organisation. We are trying to identify and negotiate funding from The Department For International Development UK (DFID) (www.dfid.gov.uk) for the new services. This is a UK government department for promoting sustainable development and reducing poverty. It is committed to the internationally agreed millennium development goals to be achieved by 2015. These seek to eradicate extreme poverty and hunger; achieve universal primary education; promote gender equality and empower women; reduce child mortality; improve maternal health; combat HIV/AIDS, malaria and other diseases; ensure environmental sustainability; and develop a global partnership for development. DFID's assistance is concentrated in the poorest countries of sub-Saharan Africa and Asia, but also contributes to poverty reduction and sustainable development in middle-income countries, including those in Latin America and Eastern Europe. Following the human resource management principle, we encourage staff to participate actively in virtually all the leadership roles.

PRINCIPLES FOR ESTABLISHING COALITIONS/COMMUNICATIONS

These include influencing/negotiating principles that are to gain cooperation from others to obtain information and accomplish goals for information work; interpersonal skills for considering and responding appropriately to the information needs, feelings, and capabilities of different people in different situations, is tactful, compassionate and sensitive, and treats others with respect; oral communication that makes clear and convincing oral presentations to individuals or groups, listens effectively and clarifies information as needed, facilitates an open exchange of ideas and fosters an atmosphere of open communication; partnering that develops networks and builds alliances, engages in cross-functional activities, collaborates across boundaries, and finds common ground with a widening range of stakeholders, utilises contacts to build and strengthen internal support bases and written communication principles that expresses facts and ideas in writing in a clear, convincing and organised manner.

With the principle of partnering calls or maintaining contacts outside the library with key stakeholders in the parent institution, in our case we have a strong liaison with the Directorate of clinical services; that's why we were able to integrate our services with the home visits team. We are part of the medical library network and share certain resources with the National Medical Library-Sir Albert Cook Library. We serve as a significant contact point with The Uganda Library Association which influences the environment in ways that are beneficial to the library also following the principle of oral communication; we share and distribute information within the library through staff meetings and personal contacts. We also invite inputs from individuals and groups within the library, listen attentively to that input and act on it for the good of the library and its users.

NOTES

1. Pro-Action for change in Research Libraries by Martha Kyrillidou. ARL and Stanley Wilder; http://www.arl.org/newsltr/208_209/proaction.html, 22/02/2003.
2. National Surveillance Annual Report on HIV/AIDS in Uganda June 2002.

REFERENCES

James, Jennifer. Thinking in the Future tense, (New, York: Touchstone, 1997).
Katzenbach, Jon R., ed. The Work of Teams. (Boston: Harvard Business School Press, 1998.)

Leveraging Natural Skills
to Overcome Traditional Ways
in a Third World Library

Foli Kuevidjen

SUMMARY. On March 1, 1985, my appointment began as the Supervisory Librarian at the American Cultural Center Library in Niamey, Niger. It operated as a reading room. In my new position, different ways were adopted to change the library's outlook. With the arrival of different directors, the library was restructured. New equipment was installed and services were offered to the general public. During the first Gulf War, the Center was attacked. The library was closed for more than a year. After relocating to a different neighborhood, outreach activities were organized to attract patrons. The library is called the "Rosa Parks Library." *[Article copies available for a fee from The Haworth Document Delivery Service: 1-800-HAWORTH. E-mail address: <docdelivery@haworthpress.com> Website: <http://www.Haworth Press.com> © 2002 by The Haworth Press, Inc. All rights reserved.]*

KEYWORDS. American Cultural Center, Niamey, Niger, supervisory librarian, Gulf War, Rosa Parks Library

Foli Kuevidjen is Head, Information Resource Center, Lome, Togo (E-mail: f_kuevidjen@fastmail.fm).

[Haworth co-indexing entry note]: "Leveraging Natural Skills to Overcome Traditional Ways in a Third World Library." Kuevidjen, Foli. Co-published simultaneously in *Science & Technology Libraries* (The Haworth Information Press, an imprint of The Haworth Press, Inc.) Vol. 23, No. 2/3, 2002, pp. 113-122; and: *Leadership and Management Principles in Libraries in Developing Countries* (ed: Wei Wei, Sue O'Neill Johnson, and Sylvia E. A. Piggott) The Haworth Information Press, an imprint of The Haworth Press, Inc., 2002, pp. 113-122. Single or multiple copies of this article are available for a fee from The Haworth Document Delivery Service [1-800-HAWORTH, 9:00 a.m. - 5:00 p.m. (EST). E-mail address: docdelivery@haworth press.com].

Digital Object Identifier: 10.1300/J122v23n02_14

On March 1, 1985, my appointment as Librarian at the American Cultural Center in Niamey, Niger came into effect. Formally, the library was known as the "Bibliothèque du Centre Culturel Américain," under the tutelage of the now-defunct United States Information Service (USIS). Niger, a French-speaking predominantly Moslem country in West Africa, lies in the path that extends from the Sahara[1] (the Arabic word for "desert") on the edges of the North African boundary that continues to the Atlantic Ocean. A paradox that confuses westerners is the fact that the same name applies to a state in the Federal Republic of Nigeria, Niger's richer eastern neighbor.

Due to its geographical location in the Sahel[2] (the Arabic word for a semiarid region), Niger becomes more dusty than usual during the dry season that commences with the blowing of the hot wind that ushers in the harmattan.[3] Generally, the season runs from October to April. The dust causes problems not found elsewhere. In April 1985, for example, there was a severe dust storm that made visibility impossible and businesses were closed on a particular day that looked like the last day on earth.

My predecessor had run the library in a traditional manner since 1964. The library lost its value and identification and, rather, became a reading room. Patrons sat at the same table and almost read the same books. It became evident that those who came to the library were students writing their final year papers. Another factor that lured the public into the library during the hot months of April through June was the single air-conditioner that kept the temperature around 82.5F (28C). If the lunar sightings made the Moslem fasting month of Ramadan coincide with the hot season, seats in the library became as precious as the manner by which movie watchers and critics reserved places for an upcoming premier of a new film in Hollywood. It was commonplace to see people sitting on the carpet with pages of books opened and sitting on their laps.

After assuming function in June of the same year, the general structure of the library was modified and basic guidelines for library use were introduced. The structural modification involved rearranging the furniture and shelves. The shelves were moved against the four walls that gave the room a square form. The chairs and tables were moved forward and they no longer stayed behind the shelves. Concerning guidelines, simple and clear rules such as leaving books on the tables and paying attention not to disturb other people were written and displayed on the tables. To implement the new regulations in an effective manner, friendly pep talks about exemplary behavior in public places were given to patrons who showed up early.

Later on, they transmitted my call to peers whenever someone in the library conducted himself in a different manner. Others were less accepting. They saw me as the "library police" because they felt that certain values that did not relate to their own traditions, culture, manners and religion were being imposed on them. Among these were asking people not to remove shoes, to come to the library equipped with pens, pencils and paper, have a defined purpose and be willing to find information and answers to questions. Also, chewing gum and pasting it under the tables was vehemently prohibited.

The warm relationship that existed between regular patrons enticed me. They took turns and shook hands with each other anytime they met in the library. Others cared about knowing why a particular person was absent. The regular patrons went beyond the scope of the library and maintained cordial contacts and even invited one another to marriage ceremonies or to gatherings when one of them had returned from the Hadj in Mecca. There were roughly ten minutes of general discussion each day to steam-off and focus on the day's objective after patrons had taken their seats. Discussions ranged from politics to the weather and even to how marriages were celebrated the previous day. At times, the discussions filled with passion had the tendency to last longer and the patrons were reminded about the quiet atmosphere that the library deserved.

Questions also came in from all sectors of the society. Pictures of landscapes and animals in the "National Geographic" monthly publication caused a sensation among casual visitors. Some even came to me at the circulation desk to enquire if it was true that Americans had really landed on the moon. A reference question that required guts and patience to answer came from a curious walk-in visitor. He wanted to know if the soil in the United States of America was different from that of Niger. He wondered about the agricultural prowess of the United States as compared to that of Niger.

A thorough inventory was conducted for the first time in many years. Titles published as far back as 1967 were still on the shelves. It took us almost three weeks to accomplish one of the most grueling tasks in our lives. Thick layers of dust filled the space between the books as well as the top because of their horizontal surface. Much time was spent on cleaning. Both of us had dry and wet fabric tissues on hand to wipe off the dust and then cleaned the books as well as the shelves. The return slips were checked and titles were also verified to make sure of each title's borrowing frequency. Several books were pulled out and were donated to public libraries as well as the University Libraries.

After a dramatic downsizing of the core collection had taken place, new titles that supported the Post's country plan were ordered–to beef up and modernize the core collection. French language titles were also added to heighten the bilingual status of the library. In an effort to turn the library into a universal place of sharing and acquiring new ideas, the Holy Koran and the Bible were ordered. One day, a mullah or an Islamic teacher came and made a self-introduction. After the formal greetings, he retorted that the Koran was not supposed to be on display, particularly in our library. He considered the Holy Koran to be sacred and that a non-Moslem should never read nor touch it and, therefore, should not be in possession of it. The undisclosed fact was that the Centre Culturel Américain could not be identified with Islam. My response was simple. When he learned that the Koran was ordered from a bookstore in the U.S., he nevertheless held to his position. One fact that marveled the mullah was to learn that the Bible existed long before the Koran. To my surprise, most of the visitors to the library referred to passages in the Bible from time to time. The Koran disappeared mysteriously from the library later.

The arrival of a new Director, David Queen to USIS-Niamey brought in new zeal and support for the library. His previous post was Islamabad in Pakistan. He put out a request and a professional designer came to assess the structure of the whole library. Her recommendations yielded good results and the library took an L-shape. Enough space was carved out for an audiovisual corner where videocassettes were viewed with earphones. The monitor faced the wall away from the reading public and viewers sat in quiet environments. The library kept video recordings of ABC News. Viewing the cassettes became popular among the patrons. Some listened to the cassettes to sharpen their English comprehension and others viewed it to keep abreast of current events. As patrons got used to library ethics, researches were performed with less guidance from me. At the beginning of my tenure, patrons expected me to do their researches for them.

Fewer girls and women came to the library to borrow or read books. To overcome the stigma of keeping women apart in Moslem societies, a "Black History Month" quiz was initiated for the first time and it took place in February of 1987. The questions were drawn from books, magazine articles and the reference collection. Half of the questions dealt with women. The responses were impressive with 30% coming from female participants. At the prize award celebration, three girls won prizes for giving good answers. Women came regularly to the library hence-forth. The library had begun to respond to women's needs more than in the past. Girls from high schools came in groups and worked on curriculum themes. They read articles in magazines such as Ebony and Essence that cover topics on women in general, how they lived and coped with social problems such as sexual harassment, rape and female emancipation in the modern world.

The presence of women in the library was encouraging to monitor. The trend continued and people were invited and gave lectures on topics of interest to the public. The library became an attractive learning place for people of all walks of life in dire need to share or swap ideas on diverse subjects. Later, people with profound knowledge in scientific and literary subjects offered to give lectures on papers that they had written. The library became, and played the role of, a meeting place for all those who wanted to learn about the U.S. and anything else from a local source. The hallway that separated the library from the entrance hosted diverse photo exhibitions. Whenever visitors came to view photos on display, they ended their tour in the library and enquired about membership and other cultural activities that the Center sponsored or organized. The library, per se, became a significant portal of U.S. values. Students also started to consider the possibility of studying in the U.S. The college catalogs were well displayed on the shelves, and videos of a few colleges were available for viewing in the collection that grew.

With an ardent desire to satisfy the needs of high-ranking patrons, a survey was conducted with the approval of top management. The copies of the Table of Contents (TOC) were sent to potential members of the Cultural Center's target audience. The selected members were among those who rarely came to the library, but always expressed the desire to get more information in their specialized subject areas. Some recipients of the TOC were gleaned from the record of those who came up with reference questions that required further assistance and searches that went beyond the walls of the library. A recipient was restricted to two articles from two magazines. This gave my assistant an opportunity to interact with the target audience. Although he manned the circulation desk very often, he played a major role in helping with the day-to-day management of the library. He kept the newspaper rack and the magazine stand current with newly received items. Advance alerts announcing new articles were sent to recipients by strictly adhering to U.S. copyright regulations.

Another mechanism used to discourage patrons from excessive requests for pages from books being copied manually or photocopied was the popularization of the free membership policy that had existed for every person. Special letters were sent to schools, and pupils were invited to visit the library in groups or individually. The United States Information Agency (USIA) came out with a bookmark that had the picture of a superman elevating physically between two towers of books, and it was captioned "Knowledge is Power." Any visitor who came to the circulation desk for information received a bookmark and was shown how to use it when reading a book. The visitors who came to the library at least departed with a leaflet that indicated the current library hours and services that were offered.

The library hours were modified with the consent of the Public Affairs Officer, to accommodate patrons and visitors during the Moslem fasting month of Ramadan which changed and took place two weeks later each year compared to the previous one. Hours on Fridays were modified to reflect the general traditional and religious beliefs that Friday, in general, was sacrosanct. On Fridays, a lady who had given birth to a set of twins (two girls) always came and sat on the pavement that separated the library from the main road across from Habou Béné,[4] the biggest market in Niger. It is a beneficial symbol and omen to give alms to twin babies on Fridays in Niger and in most of the Sahel region. Few visitors and patrons put coins in a plate placed in front of the twins. One Friday, after sliding two pieces of coin and two dated bookmarks with the caption "Knowledge is Power" into their plate, the mother of the twins looked at me and smiled. She pocketed the coins and asked if she could sell the bookmarks for extra money. She was told to keep the bookmarks and that, in the future, the twin girls will grow and become educated. When they read what was written on the bookmarks and referred to the date, they would know that when they were babies they had spent certain Fridays in front of a library and that they should rather go into a library and acquire knowledge. She smiled and thanked me. She promised that she would loyally transmit the message to them when they became educated and can read and write the white man's language as I can.

In 1990, the wind of democracy began to blow in Africa after the tumbling of the Berlin wall. Student uprisings became rampant. The civil society in Africa, for the first time, expressed their discontent through protest marches, boycotts, strikes and unrests. The library became a haven for students who wanted to avoid being involved in clashes with the police that often turned violent when passion flared up in extreme cases. Some students also came in to read while schools were closed, with the intention that when classes resumed, they would be ahead of the pack.

By mid-January in 1991, it became evident that the U.S. would go in and defend Kuwait after Iraq's invasion. The Persian Gulf War began in January of the same year; rioting students attacked the American Cultural Center in Niamey. The siege lasted for more than three hours. Vehicles of USIS staff and motorcycles were set on fire. Part of the building was also set on fire. Paradoxically, certain faces of the rioting students in the forefront of the protest march were identified in pictures taken from the first storey, and they were considered to be among the staunchest library patrons.

In the aftermath, the Cultural Center, including the library, was closed to the general public for almost two years. Day-to-day operations were carried out at the U.S. Embassy that was about 4 miles away. Three months after the attack, students were wondering if the library would re-open its doors to the general public. Relocating to a new building was problematic. Senior staff in Washington gave a firm and formal ruling that the building where the attack took place was no longer safe security-wise to accommodate any person whether American or non-American. A team of architects, technicians and security officials from Washington flew in at different times to analyze and make a practical assessment of the whole situation and confirm Washington's position on the Center's relocation and reopening.

During the closure of the library, books stayed on the shelves in their same place. At a meeting with a senior management staff from Washington and the Director of the Cultural Center, the need to allow serious library patrons to continue benefiting from the services of the library in an informal manner was stressed. Despite the closure of the library, management allowed the library staff to perform duties behind closed doors and provide reference services on minimal basis to the target audiences. Three days a week, the library staff went in quietly and provided reference services to those who came with the hope of keeping abreast of their research work. The periodical order kept on coming in spite of the recess. The library staff became a support and polyvalent unit.

In the first-ever-held seminar for journalists on "Reporting in a Democratic Environment" in June of 1991, the library staff set up a book display on journalism and democracy at the venue of the seminar. During the seminar, staff provided support services to the organizers by making photocopies of vital documentation related to the theme. The copies were ready and were distributed to the participants at all times. Our presence involved organization and providing logistics support to facilitate the efficient programming of the event. Later in August at the National Stadium, the staff also organized and managed a two-week exhibition of photographs of famous African-Americans in the history of the U.S. Many visitors came to see the photographs. The library personnel mounted a display of titles on African-Americans at the entrance of the hall that led to where the exhibition took place. Explanatory pamphlets on the theme of the exhibit were distributed to the general public. The recurring question as to the status of the library was constantly asked. Satisfaction beamed on faces when they were assured that the library would become functional once a suitable and well-secured location was found.

The staff also kept track of new titles and, once in a while, organized outreach programs such as book debates in other towns as far as Maradi.[5] Books were sent there after being pulled from our collection. The library in Maradi had a section for children that needed to be updated. The Center Library contributed to its upgrade by purchasing French language dictionaries, and the Center's head librarian spent two working days with the local staff in Maradi to enhance the overall structure and collection in its library. In Niamey, the Center's library increased its outreach activities by visits to schools, and supported the promotion of a visiting dramatist from Nigeria who imitated the late Rev. Dr. Martin Luther King, Jr., in his famous speech "I Have A Dream." After the sketches, the discussions highlighted non-violent and peaceful strategies to attain positive results. Participation in these programs was encouraging and the repeated question as to when the library would open its doors came from different lips. They were reminded by a single word–"soon." In mid-1992, a new location was found and repair work began on the building. Security beefing was a major concern, so the original layout of the building was modified and preventive measures were included in the restructuring process. The work lasted for almost ten months.

In February of 1993, the library was formally open to the general public. In a low-keyed ceremony, the mayor of Niamey and officials from the Ministry of Culture were invited to the ribbon-cutting ceremony. In a speech, the mayor reminded those present that the library is the best second home for anyone who strives to retrieve information and knowledge. The students were first to visit it. The setup was totally different from the former. The new library was attractive, cleaner and well spaced to accommodate patrons.

The vital change that generated a new reading explosion was the naming of the library. Upon the recommendation from the Public Affairs Officer, Mrs. Claudia Anyaso, the library was commissioned as the "Rosa Parks Library." The name had a significant meaning for the employees of the American Cultural Center. Rosa Parks is a living legend and furthermore, her name portrayed the message that the library will not succumb to attacks and menace from those who should benefit from its use. The students came to realize that their past action had deprived them of a library. An interlibrary loan program was established through the auspices of the Regional Librarian who was based in Abidjan, in Côte d'Ivoire. The "Rosa Parks Library" sent books as far as to peaceful Monrovia in Liberia in those days.

In April of 1994, to attract more people, the Rosa Parks Library organized a contest to celebrate "Earth Day" and the theme focused on how to improve the environment. Contestants were invited to come and write a two-page, one-and-a-half hour paper on the topic of their choice selected from five questions. The contest was aimed at boosting imagination and originality, and to nurture motivation and initiative. The judges were gleaned from the library's membership listing. The five judges from diverse backgrounds, ranging from environmental science to sociology, read the papers that were written and gave their individual rulings and marks. After a reckoning session at which grades and comments were reconciled, the winner and the two runner-ups were selected. In preparation for the award ceremony, coffee-table books were ordered as prizes to be distributed to all the contestants.

On April 22, the grand finale took place in the yard of the new American Cultural Center. Cash award prizes went to the lucky winners. The invited guests, including students, massively showed up for the occasion. Each participating school was asked to write one letter of the alphabet with a green background color on a plain sheet of paper. The green color symbolizes the earth. A student representing each school came forward and displayed the letter. In another quiz-like manner, the sentence that echoed the message for the special occasion was displayed to the public. In French, it is "Sauvons la Terre"–Let us Save the Earth.

To modernize routine duties and procedures in the Rosa Parks Library, Winnebago library automation software was installed. The index cards that existed in the past were completely pulled out. Checking out and returning books became just a mouse click away. More questions were answered by telephone than in the past due to the relocation. The patrons, henceforth, found the value and the necessity of a library despite its remoteness from the center of Niamey. Another reference question that came in right after the 1991 U.S. presidential elections focused on the president-elect.[6] We had distributed brief background brochures of the major contestants to the general public during the election night event. An elderly person walked to me and needed confirmation that the president-elect really had only one child. After confirmation, he left shaking his head in disillusionment about a president having a single child. He had originally thought that the president-elect would by definition be rich and, thus, by virtue of his position, should not be a parent to a single child.

At the end of the first inventory at the new site, the library staff realized that more current popular titles were missing. After cross-checking with the membership catalog, it was found that most addresses and alternative contact addresses were fictitious. The conclusion was that visitors became members only with the intent to take away a book that they found to be of particular interest. Another school of thought considered it logical to assume that lost and stolen books from the library would be in the hands of those who would at least read and make use of them.

Today, the Rosa Parks Library operates by appointment only because of the new direction that Public Affairs libraries have taken. Security concerns have become paramount in the daily operation of publicly accessed places such as the library in Niamey, Niger. The State Department-sponsored libraries in the sub-region have become reference centers with the purpose of serving a well-defined target audience with clearly outlined objectives. The human warmth that went beyond bounds to the exchange of cola nuts in order to keep a patron awake is missing, but the Internet will help bridge the gap between the library and its patrons in the years to come. Hopefully in the years to come, to encourage young people to read, more libraries will be built and a yearly budget set aside to buy books and electronic equipment such as computers and CDs. The future generation will thus be better off in coping with the dangers that haunt the human race with ills ranging from terror to child abuse, female mutilation, child trafficking and HIV/AIDS.

NOTES

1. Arabic *Sahara*, "desert." The largest tropical and climatic desert in the world.

2. Arabic *sahil*, "semiarid." The semiarid region of western Africa extends from Senegal to the Sudan.

3. The wind that blows from the northeast in the Southern Sahara mainly in winter that carries large amounts of dust which it transports hundreds of kilometers out over the Atlantic.

4. Literally means "the market situated on a hill" in Djerma, a native language spoken in Niger.

5. Maradi is the commercial capital of Niger. It is situated about 500 kilometers east of Niamey.

6. The President-elect after the 1991 U.S. presidential elections was Bill Clinton.

Library and Information Services (LIS) Strategic Planning in a Developing Country: A Case Study

Paiki Muswazi

SUMMARY. The article discusses a strategic planning initiative at the University of Swaziland Libraries. It describes the steps followed and the consultation and communication techniques used and notes the limited progress made in implementing the plan and the underlying reasons. It also critiques the reactive nature of the planning process; lack of representation of the faculty of Health Sciences and students; staff turnover; multi-faceted objectives; concurrent development of management systems and the implementation process; and inadequate funding. It concludes that a feasible LIS strategic plan in a developing country should include all stakeholder interests, while being mindful of the physical and fiscal resource and systems realities. *[Article copies available for a fee from The Haworth Document Delivery Service: 1-800-HAWORTH. E-mail address: <docdelivery@haworthpress.com> Website: <http://www.HaworthPress.com> © 2002 by The Haworth Press, Inc. All rights reserved.]*

Paiki Muswazi, MLIS, BA (Hons), Diploma in Training Management and Diploma in Personnel Management, is Head of Special Collections, University of Swaziland Libraries, Kwaluseni, Swaziland (E-mail: paiki@uniswacc.uniswa.sz or pmuswazi@ yahoo.com).

[Haworth co-indexing entry note]: "Library and Information Services (LIS) Strategic Planning in a Developing Country: A Case Study." Muswazi, Paiki. Co-published simultaneously in *Science & Technology Libraries* (The Haworth Information Press, an imprint of The Haworth Press, Inc.) Vol. 23, No. 2/3, 2002, pp. 123-133; and: *Leadership and Management Principles in Libraries in Developing Countries* (ed: Wei Wei, Sue O'Neill Johnson, and Sylvia E. A. Piggott) The Haworth Information Press, an imprint of The Haworth Press, Inc., 2002, pp. 123-133. Single or multiple copies of this article are available for a fee from The Haworth Document Delivery Service [1-800-HAWORTH, 9:00 a.m. - 5:00 p.m. (EST). E-mail address: docdelivery@haworthpress.com].

http://www.haworthpress.com/web/STL
© 2002 by The Haworth Press, Inc. All rights reserved.
Digital Object Identifier: 10.1300/J122v23n02_15

KEYWORDS. University of Swaziland Libraries, strategic planning, library and information services, mission statement, information technology, management development

BACKGROUND

LIS providers have long accepted the utility of concepts such as strategic planning that have roots in business management. A search for "strategic plan" from the *Information Science Plus*, March 2002 CD-ROM yielded 111 citations, whereas a complementary search from the 1998 print issues of *Library and Information Science Abstracts (LISA)* gave six citations. Most citations related to experiences in libraries in the developed world, notably North America. Only two citations, covering Ghana (Badu, 1997) and South Africa (Willemse, 1989), related to Africa. The Ghana case study focuses on external influences to strategic planning. The South African example discusses the formulation and application of concrete goals and objective performance measures to the document-delivery service at the University of South Africa. Overall, information and knowledge on African LIS strategic planning experiences seem not readily available and, by implication, lessons from there are apparently not widely shared.

OBJECTIVES

This article seeks to extend the discourse on African LIS strategic planning, using the University of Swaziland Libraries (UNISWA) Strategic Plan, 1999/2000-2004/2005 as a case study. The objectives are to:

- Describe the conditions under which the strategic planning process was conceived;
- Describe the application of strategic planning principles at UNISWA;
- Critique the process to take account of the factors internal to UNISWA; and
- Draw lessons from the UNISWA experience.

DATA COLLECTION

This article draws on correspondence, minutes, and reports of the UNISWA Libraries Strategic Planning Sub-Committee (LSPSC) and UNISWA Libraries Strategic Planning Implementation Sub-Committee (LSPISC); and on the author's experiences as:

- Secretary of the LSPSC, with responsibility for performing administrative tasks, participating in LSPSC meetings, recording LSPSC proceedings, and collating all submissions to the LSPSC; and
- Representing Special Collections interests at the LSPSC and the LSPISC meetings.

CONTEXT

The University of Swaziland is located in the Kingdom of Swaziland, Southern Africa, and comprises three campuses: Kwaluseni, main campus; Luyengo, agricultural campus; and Mbabane, health sciences campus. Largely funded by the central government, it offers degrees in Agriculture, Commerce, Education, Health Sciences, Humanities, Science and Social Sciences. In academic year 2002/2003, the total enrollment was 4,457.

Recently, HIV/AIDS and recurrent drought have strained the national fiscus, with adverse effects on the funding of university programs, including library and information services. Yet, new programs are being introduced, student enrollment continues to increase, and public expectations are high. It is against this background that the University embarked on strategic planning. The process commenced with the formation of a University Strategic Planning Committee (USPC) in 1998. The committee requested faculties and service departments to form strategic-planning subcommittees to deliberate and make submissions. The library strategic-planning process was a response to this university-wide initiative. On 6th February 1998, the USPC held a seminar for all the strategic-planning subcommittees at which core concepts and principles were discussed and agreed upon.

THE UNISWA LIBRARIES STRATEGIC PLANNING PROCESS

This article adapts the strategic-planning elements and model propounded by Birdsall and Hensley (1994) and the approach used by Jacobson and Sparks (2001) to analyze the UNISWA Libraries process. The elements include:

1. Establishment of the planning team;
2. Definition of the mission statement and objectives;
3. Environmental scanning;

4. Enabling strategies;
5. Benchmarking;
6. Budgeting;
7. Review and evaluation mechanisms;
8. Acceptance of the plan; and
9. Implementation.

Establishment of the Planning Team

A key element in strategic planning is to staff the team with those people who best represent areas of major impact. At UNISWA, a Library Strategic Planning Sub-Committee (LSPSC) of five was formed representing library core functions: library top management, technical services, special collections, readers' services, and the Agriculture library. The acting university librarian chaired the committee and the author provided secretarial services.

Definition of the Mission Statement and Objectives

A strategic plan requires a clearly defined mission statement. At a marketing seminar held in May 1996, the library defined its mission: "To support instructional, teaching, learning and research functions of the University Community through the efficient provision of information resources and services."

The LSPSC decided that this statement did not sufficiently address the "quality" and "stakeholder" components, and decided to review it. The LSPSC consulted library professional and paraprofessional staff, library top management, and the Library Senate Committee. In addition, it sought inspiration from the strategic plans of the University of Botswana Library, the Thomas Mofolo Library (National University of Lesotho), and the Copperbelt University Library (Zambia). It also examined the mission statements of various libraries that are accessible on the Internet.

These efforts resulted in a revised mission statement: "To efficiently provide services and access to quality academic information resources, irrespective of format and location, to university staff, students and associates in support of instructional, learning, research and administrative functions of the university."

Subsequently, the LSPSC requested that library staff identify strategic issues and define the objectives of the library within the framework of the revised mission statement. All submissions were consolidated to create a list of ten strategic issues and 12 objectives. The issues included information technology, physical infrastructure, policies and procedures, collaboration, funding, management, human resources development, preservation, marketing, and information service delivery.

Environmental Scanning

An environmental scan identifies areas that advance the mission statement. Ideally, the information should be solicited from library staff, university management, faculty, and students. At UNISWA, the LSPSC consulted with only professional and para-professional library staff, resulting in the identification of six strengths, ten weaknesses, three opportunities, and two threats.

Notwithstanding the preponderance of weaknesses, the scanning exercise helped the library recognize the strengths of its qualified professionals and in its collaborative resource-sharing arrangements, and the opportunities presented by its Internet connectivity.

Enabling Strategies

Any consideration of strategic options should result in development of the most appropriate strategies for meeting the goals and objectives and dealing with the issues raised in the environmental scan. The LSPSC considered each strategic issue in the light of the relevant strategic objectives, and developed 25 enabling strategies.

Benchmarking

The design of a strategic plan requires a measurement system to gauge progress in attaining objectives. UNISWA adopted a simplified approach for identifying and linking milestones to strategic issues, objectives, and enabling strategies. This activity resulted in 65 benchmarks, with a time line spanning the period 2000 to 2005.

Financial Plan

Implementation of a strategic plan requires funding. Thus, all items required to action the benchmarks were identified and priced, resulting in a total budget of E48 169 000,00[1] spread over the 2000/2001 to 2004/2005 period.

Review and Evaluation Mechanisms

One result of the university-wide strategic-planning process was that the University Planning Center (UPC) was established to monitor and advise on implementation of the plan. The UPC in turn requested that the Faculties and Service departments appoint plan-implementation teams. To this end, the LSPSC was restructured to form a Libraries Strategic Planning Implementation Sub-Committee (LSPISC), chaired by the university librarian, and comprised of the deputy librarian and head of Readers' Services; the heads of Acquisitions, the Agriculture Library, Cataloguing, the Health Sciences Library, Serials (who also served as secretary to the committee), and Special Collections. The LSPISC is required to submit quarterly progress reports to the UPC for the information of university management.

Acceptance of the Plan

To secure support in the allocation of scarce resources, all stakeholders should accept the strategic plan. As the plan for the libraries evolved, it received input and endorsement from library staff, the Library Senate Committee, and the University Strategic Planning Committee. To this extent, it is an accepted document; indeed, the University Senate and Council officially adopted the strategic plan for implementation.

In all, it took over 16 meetings, from February 1998 to September 2000, to come up with the UNISWA Libraries Strategic Plan, 1999/2000-2004/2005 (University of Swaziland Libraries, 2000) before it was adopted for implementation.

IMPLEMENTATION

A review of progress on the 12 strategic objectives, the related 25 enabling strategies, and the 65 benchmarks shows that by the beginning of 2003, the following actions had been taken.

Information Technology

- During 2002, space was identified and cabled at the Kwaluseni Campus library to widen Internet access; however, the shortage of computer equipment has delayed the use of the facility.

- The library secured subscription funding from the Open Society Institute (OSI), enabling it to provide user access to the *EBSCO Host* full-text databases during the year 2002. Anticipating expiration of OSI's sponsorship in 2003, the UNISWA libraries hosted a workshop in October 2002 to kick-start the formation of a national consortium to facilitate the pooling of resources and enable the continuation of *EBSCO Host* subscriptions in 2003 and beyond. A steering committee chaired by the university librarian was formed to lead the establishment of the consortium.
- Following an application by the library in 2001, the Rockefeller Foundation funded subscription to the 1993-1996 CD ROM base set of *The Essential Electronic Agricultural Library* (TEEAL) database, thereby giving users access to quality bibliographic and full-text information on agriculture, beginning in 2003.
- Efforts at giving users access to freely available quality Internet resources took off with the design and provision of the *Geography, Environment and Planning Information Gateway (GEPIG)* link collection by the author (Muswazi, 2002) and the free full text journals link collection by the Serials Librarian (Anbu, 2002). The link collections were accessible from the UNISWA libraries website at <http://library.uniswa.sz>, beginning in November 2002.
- Five personal computers, five video cameras, seven videocassette recorders, and one overhead projector were purchased in 2002 to enrich the instructional, teaching, learning, research, and administrative functions of the university. However, lack of suitably qualified technical support staff hinders optimal utilization of the equipment.

Physical Infrastructure

Library facilities at the Luyengo agricultural campus were upgraded and extended in 2001.

Management

At the first meeting of the LSPISC, held on 21st May 2002, members were each asked to draft terms of reference for the formation of Library Links, Budget, Staffing, Preservation (the author was given this responsibility), and Information Service Delivery sub-committees to lead the implementation of strategies relating to these key issues.

By and large, only a limited number of the benchmarks had been realized at the beginning of 2003.

COMMENTARY

From the onset, the LSPSC realized the importance of communication in getting all staff on board. The LSPSC regularly issued memoranda inviting submissions and giving feedback. Drafts of collated input were exchanged between staff and LSPSC for comments. Some departments convened meetings to agree on inputs to the LSPSC, whereas others adopted a more laissez faire approach, with individual staff members making independent written submissions to the LSPSC. In addition, LSPSC members informally collected fringe ideas not expressed in the written input. Overall, library responses to the USPC were prompt, which helped boost morale. These communication techniques helped underpin this invaluable consultative process.

The pressure to produce a credible plan was considerable. The LSPSC recognized that paraprofessional staff working at the front end have deep insight into operational issues. Their views were deliberately solicited, and these served to validate as well as challenge ideas advanced by professional staff. This collaboration contributed substantially to the validity of the plan and to imparting a sense of legitimacy. On the other hand, the overall direction given by university top management meant that the process proceeded on a reactive basis, affecting the plan's originality. (For example, the library felt constrained to do contingency planning for some critical items, such as the acquisition of additional land for a new library at Mbabane, which it felt would be best handled at a university-wide level.)

The interests of the faculty of Health Sciences and of student users were not directly represented on the LSPSC; however, it should be noted that there were no senior personnel in the faculty of Health Sciences. While these same interests were represented indirectly at the higher levels of the Library Senate Committee, and University Senate and Council, the lack of input from Health Sciences and students to the LSPSC, where the spadework occurred, militated against the production of an all-inclusive plan.

The strategic-planning process was subject to intense intellectual debate. It took three years (February 1998 to October 2000) to agree on and adopt the plan. This is understandable in the context of the academic setting in which the process occurred. Unquestionably, the extensive sharing of ideas ensured some relative depth of coverage. At the same time, prolonged analysis threatened to cloud the ultimate ends: production, implementation, and review of the plan. It also left little room for thinking through implementation mechanisms. (For instance, the plan identifies the criticality of management development to leading the required changes in service provision; however, concerted actions in this regard were rare.) Evidently, the strategic-planning process was a learning experience for most participants. The pressure to implement the plan–while at the same time developing strategy implementation and performance-review systems–apparently impeded the transition from planning to implementation. Thus, the implementation pace and reporting frequency expected by the UPC and by the LSPISC were not in synchrony.

Substantive progress in attaining strategic objectives is partly dependent on funding. A comparison of the strategic-plan budget estimates and actual allocations since the beginning of implementation are shown in Table 1.

Table 1 shows that funding of the library plan is inadequate. Traditionally, library programs are funded centrally by the over-stretched university administration. Although nothing would prevent the library from independently sourcing funds, and it has indeed taken the initiative in some instances, there apparently is a perception that fundraising is a centralized university administration responsibility. The strategic planning experience did not sufficiently debunk this perception. As a consequence, neither the university administration nor the library can guarantee adequate funding for all the library strategies.

Furthermore, the planning environment was characterized by library staff turnover. During the three-year planning process, three senior members of staff resigned (two of them had been members of LSPSC) and new appointments made. New staff brought fresh perspectives to the planning process; the major drawback was that this required more time to bring them up to speed and possibly eroded the team's sense of ownership.

Ultimately, the implementation of the plan was/has been influenced by the concurrent development of management systems and the imple-

TABLE 1. Library Strategic-Plan Budget

Year	Estimate (E)	Actual allocation (E)	Shortfall (E)
2000/2001*	7 303 000,00	1 518 000,00	5 722 000,00
2001/2002	7 321 000,00	960 000,00	6 361 000,00
2002/2003	7 575 000,00	960 000,00	6 615 000,00

*Due to delays in producing the plan, the initial implementation commencement target date of 1999/2000 was postponed to 2000/2001.

mentation process, which seems to overwhelm staff as they go through the learning experience; and inadequate funding.

LESSONS

Commendable Approaches

- A combination of written and informal communication channels proved important in producing an informed and commonly shared plan.
- At both LSPSC and staff levels, everybody was given a chance to be heard. Collecting the views of paraprofessional operational staff and policy-oriented professionals resulted in a plan that is closer to reality, at least from the viewpoint of the planners, although not necessarily user groups.

What Could Have Been Done Better?

In hindsight, the planning exercise did not pay sufficient attention to the significance of user involvement, manageable objectives, management development, and management systems. A robust strategic plan should have inbuilt mechanisms to prevent any loss of momentum at implementation. Issues to consider include:

- The planning committee over relied on formal administrative structures, rather than at least partly recruiting its membership from grass roots student and faculty user groups. This should have mobilized sufficient user group interest in the plan. In turn, user groups advocacy can help keep the pressure on and push for implementation of strategies that address their own library and information needs.
- The objectives, strategies and benchmarks were unwieldy. A streamlined list is more practical than a long, detailed list. The strategic planning process should address the financial and personnel realities of implementing LIS in a developing country.
- Embarking on LIS strategic planning in a developing country should be accompanied by implementation of a management-development program, so as to further sharpen the team's planning, implementation, and review competencies.
- Corresponding/enabling management systems must be readily available to facilitate implementation processes. A conscious effort should be made to enhance the administrative instruments as an integral part of the planning process.

CONCLUSION

The academic environment in which the UNISWA Libraries' strategic plan was conceived resulted in a document that is relatively deep in content; however, insufficient representation of user interests and limited attention to implementation logistics impacted on the practicality of the plan. To a large extent, inadequate funding of the cumbersome multifaceted objectives constitutes a major challenge to staff abilities to implement the plan. In the final analysis, a feasible LIS strategic plan in a developing country should include all stakeholder interests, while being mindful of the physical and fiscal resource and systems realities.

REFERENCES

Anbu, K.J.P. *Free Online Journals*, 2002. Available: <http://library.uniswa.sz/i.htm>. [accessed: 30 Jan. 2003].

Badu, E.E. "Strategic Planning in an Uncertain Environment: the Case of Ghana's University Libraries." *Information Development*, 13, no. 4 (Dec. 1997): 173-178.

Birdsall, Douglas G. and Hensley, Oliver D. "A New Strategic Planning Model for Academic Libraries." *College & Research Libraries*, 55, no. 2 (Mar. 1994): 149-159.

Jacobson, Alvin L. and Sparks, JoAnne L. "Creating Value: Building the Strategy-Focused Library." *Information Outlook*, 5, no. 9 (Sept. 2001): 14-20.

Muswazi, Paiki. *Geography, Environment and Planning Information Gateway (GEPIG)*, 2002. Available: <http://library.uniswa.sz/gepighome.htm>. [accessed: 30 Jan. 2003].

University of Swaziland Libraries. *Strategic Plan1999/2000-2004/2005*. In: University of Swaziland. *Strategic Plan: UNISWA's Commitment to Self-Renewal, 1999/2000-2004/2005*. Kwaluseni: The University, 2000.

Willemse, John. "Library Effectiveness–the Need for Measurement." *South African Journal of Library and Information Science*, 57, no. 3 (Sept. 1989): 261-266.

NOTE

1. E = Emalangeni, the Swaziland currency. US$1,00 = E9,00.

The Application of Leadership
and Management Principles and Strategies
in an Information Resource Center
in Burkina Faso

Josephine Ouedraogo

SUMMARY. Nowadays, people discovered that management principles and leadership strategies applied to an information service works as well as an enterprise which makes a profit. In Burkina Faso, an Information Resources Center that we worked at applied these principles and strategies. Working to improve the information, using an adequate policy of acquisition, getting close with the users and considering their needs, innovating, and communicating allowed this information service to improve the quality of the information, attract many patrons, and raise the image of the institution. *[Article copies available for a fee from The Haworth Document Delivery Service: 1-800-HAWORTH. E-mail address: <docdelivery@haworthpress.com> Website: <http://www.HaworthPress.com> © 2002 by The Haworth Press, Inc. All rights reserved.]*

KEYWORDS. Information resources center, management principles, leadership, strategies, Burkina Faso

Josephine Ouedraogo is Information Resource Center Technician, American Embassy, 10 BP 13661 Ouagadougou, 10 Burkina Faso (E-mail: ouedraj@ hotmail.com).

[Haworth co-indexing entry note]: "The Application of Leadership and Management Principles and Strategies in an Information Resource Center in Burkina Faso." Ouedraogo, Josephine. Co-published simultaneously in *Science & Technology Libraries* (The Haworth Information Press, an imprint of The Haworth Press, Inc.) Vol. 23, No. 2/3, 2002, pp. 135-138; and: *Leadership and Management Principles in Libraries in Developing Countries* (ed: Wei Wei, Sue O'Neill Johnson, and Sylvia E. A. Piggott) The Haworth Information Press, an imprint of The Haworth Press, Inc., 2002, pp. 135-138. Single or multiple copies of this article are available for a fee from The Haworth Document Delivery Service [1-800-HAWORTH, 9:00 a.m. - 5:00 p.m. (EST). E-mail address: docdelivery@haworthpress.com].

Digital Object Identifier: 10.1300/J122v23n02_16

In the past, people thought that leadership and management were only oriented to companies and business enterprises that make a profit. But as time flies by, they noticed that leadership and management principles can be applied to a library which doesn't make a profit. We will state here the experiences that we lived in our professional life. These experiences are based on the product and the patrons, the innovation we brought, the communication techniques and the lessons we have learned.

Before we worked for the Information Resource Center, we worked six years in a scientific research institute as a librarian. When we started in this Information Service, there was a lot to do and we didn't know where to start. Our mission was to manage this service as a professional and promote the image of this institution by disseminating the results of the research, which is contained in the books published by the researchers. After deep reflection, we had a meeting to think together on the ways to develop the product the information offered, to promote the institute's image, to advertise and communicate, to innovate and have everybody satisfied. So we decided to start by promoting the product: the information contained in the books.

THE PRODUCT

This institute had a lot of materials with relevant information but this information was not well processed. Patrons were not satisfied at all. The database was like an e-mail box full of junk. The staff responsible for the Information Center were not trained in information science, and were working without any policy to develop their service, nor were any motivated. We realized that we cannot reach the patrons without offering them appropriate and relevant information. The first battle was to review the database, clean it, delete duplicates, review every field respecting the cataloguing and the indexation. As a lot of materials were stocked waiting to be processed, we processed them and entered them in the database. To protect the database, we created files in which we had to enter the new acquisitions and process them. Periodically, we transferred the contents of these files into the database after making the necessary corrections. We also worked with the computer technician to create interfaces that allow patrons to search in the database. Then we baptized the database and we also initiated training for the users. To provide further help in addition to the training, we wrote down the steps to search in an easy and an advanced way and posted them near each computer. This was a success and the training provided attracted many of our patrons to the Information Center.

Another issue we would like to point out is that we specified the product. The institute is a scientific research institute and we defined the information we want to disseminate: only scientific information. Therefore, we oriented our order and purchased only scientific material and this led us to work closely with the users.

THE PATRONS

We had two types of patrons: the internal patrons and the external patrons. We decided to work first with the internal patrons who are the researchers. We initiated a meeting with them and engaged them in ordering materials according to their field. The subscriptions to scientific magazines followed the same principles. When we received magazines, we circulated them among the researchers; they ticked off the articles they wanted us to catalog, index and enter in the database. They appreciated this approach and we reviewed their profiles too. To keep them informed, we used to send them the bibliography of the new acquisitions.

For the external patrons, we decided to make a survey. We wanted to see what is the image of our information service that external patrons have. The results of the survey was that we organized more training sessions, we increased the open days, and we opened a photocopy service.

We also used to post the front pages of every new material on a board in front of the Information Service and this also served to inform the patrons.

INNOVATION

Sometime later when we had the appropriate technology, we decided to open an Internet room. Burkina Faso is a developing country and many people do not understand the Internet. We invited the university teachers, the journalists, the members of parliament and the government to come use the Information Center's Internet for their research. Here again, we had to train people on the use of the Internet.

At the dedication of this Internet room, we took advantage and organized an open house. We invited all our patrons and all our key contacts. We set up a PowerPoint presentation on the information service, presented the collection (materials, CD-ROMs, magazines), our goals and mission, how one can become a member and what service we offer. We took the visitors on many tours of the service. We also had Internet training sessions. This was a big success for us, because this special day increased the number of our patrons.

Another innovation was when we decided to aggressively market our services to some key persons in our community with information. We opened a record of key persons working for the government, the parliament, the Non Governmental Organizations, the religious leaders, the journalists, the political parties and the human rights activists specific web sites and search for information in their field. And when we found a relevant article, we edited it and sent it by e-mail when the person has an e-mail address, otherwise by messenger. The feedback on this service was good.

COMMUNICATION

The communication strategy we developed is based on four points. We mentioned a board in front of the information service. We posted the front pages of the new acquisitions but also any information that can help the patrons, for instance the open days and the access hours. We created a pamphlet of the information service and we distributed it to the new patrons. We also inserted information about the service on the institute's web site in the Internet so that people can discover it. We tried to participate in the national association of librarians activities and at each opportunity, we introduced our center.

We also use the intranet to inform the researchers and the colleagues of any news about the information service. This also helped a lot.

LESSONS LEARNED

Librarianship or Documentation is a very important and interesting job. Information is power and when one holds it he is powerful. We also understood that an information service should have an adequate budget to run all the activities which and to promote the image of the service. When there is no budget it is difficult to work properly. We have learned we have to position the Information service, to convince head persons that it is important to support Information Resources Center with an adequate funding so that it can carry out its mandate.

Finally, we also learned that the Information service staff should work as a team and keep one objective: buy into the goals and objectives of the Information Center, and offer a useful and qualified professional product. Staff should also periodically update their knowledge through training, be motivated by the front office.

The Application of Leadership and Management Principles and Strategies to an Information Service– The British Council Management Information Centre, Mombasa

Mary N. Stevens

SUMMARY. The promotion and development of leadership and management principles with our target audiences is a major focus of our activities in British Council Mombasa. The British Council is committed to supporting the Africa-led programme New Partnership for Africa's Development, NEPAD, which aims to promote sustainable development in Africa through better leadership and governance. This is being done through the support of the reform agenda of transformational leadership and more engagement with young potential future leaders. The Council provides them with a platform that they can use to develop leadership and management skills. The Management Forum is one such platform and is the one discussed in this paper. The Management Forum is an association of managers in the region who have come together with the main aim of providing a channel through which managers across all professions and industries could share their experience and exchange information. They

Mary N. Stevens is Manager, British Council, Mombasa Management Center and Chair, Kenya National Library Services Board, P.O. Box 95795 Mombasa, Kenya (E-mail: Mary.Stevens@britishcouncil.or.ke).

[Haworth co-indexing entry note]: "The Application of Leadership and Management Principles and Strategies to an Information Service–The British Council Management Information Centre, Mombasa." Stevens, Mary N. Co-published simultaneously in *Science & Technology Libraries* (The Haworth Information Press, an imprint of The Haworth Press, Inc.) Vol. 23, No. 2/3, 2002, pp. 139-144; and: *Leadership and Management Principles in Libraries in Developing Countries* (ed: Wei Wei, Sue O'Neill Johnson, and Sylvia E. A. Piggott) The Haworth Information Press, an imprint of The Haworth Press, Inc., 2002, pp. 139-144. Single or multiple copies of this article are available for a fee from The Haworth Document Delivery Service [1-800-HAWORTH, 9:00 a.m. - 5:00 p.m. (EST). E-mail address: docdelivery@haworthpress.com].

work to provide networking opportunities for one another, influence management thinking through creating awareness of good practice, capacity building of their institutions and individuals and also recognise excellence in management through awards. The Forum is governed by a code of ethics. The paper looks at one specific activity of the forum, which is to organise management conventions/forums–a platform for managers to come together and deliberate on an issue that concerns them. This was the first convention organised and I happened to be in the centre of it. Hence my writing this paper to discuss my involvement in the process. *[Article copies available for a fee from The Haworth Document Delivery Service: 1-800-HAWORTH. E-mail address: <docdelivery@haworthpress.com> Website: <http://www.HaworthPress.com>*

KEYWORDS. British Council work in Mombasa, NEPAD–new partnership for Africa's development management forum, conventions–as a platform for discussion with target audience

A major focus for the British Council in Kenya is management. This focus is part of the 2005 strategy for the British Council world-wide. I joined the British Council in May 2000 as the Mombasa Information Centre manager. I arrived just in time to start the implementation of the 2005 strategy.

"The Mombasa Information Centre" is one of three British Council offices in Kenya, and is located 500 km from the headquarters in Nairobi and 1,000 km from the Kisumu office. Though I was very new, I was to take part in a restructuring exercise for both the office and the staff. At that time, the office offered education information to its target audience, having changed from a lending library service three years before that. Staff to fit the new management focus had to be recruited. The client base was to change also, and I would have to identify and approach the new target audience. I love challenges and this offered a double challenge for me. This was a case of change management and I have enjoyed it–both the challenge it posed and the opportunity to be part of the change process.

Before joining the British Council I worked in the management development sector, working with development agencies in management training for small and medium business enterprises. My work was geared to enhancing managerial competencies and designing business growth strategies. This was a big challenge because it was during a period of economic down turn in Kenya–from 1997 to 2000.

Our first task at the Management Centre was to define the target audience. This was not too difficult because a country strategy paper was in place that indicated who the target for the management focus would be. Identifying the potential target audience in my region was not too difficult either, as it was comprised of the same people that I had worked with in my previous jobs.

HOW THE CENTRE EVOLVED INTO A MANAGEMENT CENTER

I worked with the team of two in the office to organize the first focus day, which was aimed at discussing with our potential clients what we planned to do. During the focus day we emphasized that we were looking for partners like themselves to achieve those objectives. We wanted strategic partners who identified with our ideas and were willing to work with us through the process. Many issues came up related to expected support and collaboration. The best outcome was the willingness on the part of our target audience to collaborate.

However, not all was smooth sailing. Some participants who attended the focus evening wanted to know why the British Council had changed its focus from providing the general lending library services that they enjoyed. They wanted to know why they could not have the library back instead. This question recurred long after the focus evening.

During the focus group session, the benefits of the new management services being offered were clearly stated to the target audience. I felt that I was successful in getting this because I had a good working relationship with a majority of the people in the audience from previous encounters. At this time I realised, however, that there comes a point in a career when easy answers and service analysis alone are no longer sufficient. I felt challenged to think deeply, clearly and globally. This situation, with a terrific audience who both probed and encouraged, helped me to become an even better management thinker. Every encounter with this group has been stimulating, challenging, at times humorous and always an important part of my learning environment.

From this point on, I started to develop working relationships with our target group. We invited them to become members of our Management Centre and also asked them to assist in the selection of text materials to stock at our center. These resources were part of the member benefits provided by the British Council. We had already agreed that the members could best identify resources they needed in various aspects of their work

Within the same year, 2000, during one of our focus meetings, members expressed a desire to hold a forum at which they could get to know one another, network and share experiences, and learn from each other and from other role models they identified to come speak to them. This brought about the start of the Management Forum, which is made up of British Council Centre members. The Forum is independent of the Centre, but the Centre works as a partner with this group to advance both British Council and Forum objectives.

A long-term goal for both is to see the Management Forum grow into a national and an East and Central Africa regional forum, if not an African forum, with the British Council serving as a partner through its Africa regional offices. This would complement NEPAD, which is viewed as an African initiative. The African-driven NEPAD also works to foster economic and political development. To complement the Management Forum, I have initiated a legal networking event across East Africa, which already has government to government co-operation in their parliamentary assembly. This offers a cross-border network for enhanced sharing of business experiences.

One major event I would like to highlight was the organization of a management convention for 100 participants in February 2003. This initiative came about as a challenge from my Regional Director, Peter Elborn, who felt we had formed a good partnership with the managers in the region and had successfully established a forum for networking. I took on this challenge in May 2002, enlisted the interest and commitment of Forum members, and together started to organize the event. This was not an easy task as Forum members were committed to their full-time work elsewhere and could not concentrate on this event–it was not on the top of their priority lists.

The other challenge was that 2002 was election year for Kenya. The elections were to take place two months before the convention. For the first time in 24 years, Kenya was to constitutionally choose a new President. This was a new breed of politics for Kenyans. It was no wonder therefore, that everyone was swept up in three to four months of campaign fever, including our Management Forum members. Campaign fever did not help me either, but neither did it stop my enthusiasm to succeed. This was partly because I had suggested the theme chosen for the convention: "Shaping the Future–Which Way for Kenya?" and this theme was becoming more appropriate as election fever increased. My reason for picking this theme was because, as a civil society lobbyist and advocate in my previous work, before joining the British Council, I saw how the country's economy was deteriorating. Things were getting tougher for the common person. I realized that managers could combine their abilities, get involved and engage in the development of the country in a proactive way. I saw the convention as a call to all managers in our region to come together to find lasting solutions to enormous social, economic and political challenges and problems. This would be an opportunity to challenge ourselves as managers, to think of the great things we could contribute almost effortlessly for the region. I felt we had a role to play as the major stakeholders and an opportunity that we could not afford to leave to chance any more.

In January, after a fairly smooth election that ushered in the change desired by the majority of citizens, it was time to work aggressively to get the final convention preparations underway. The Convention took place as scheduled, on 18 February 2003. We had excellent speakers including the British Higher Commissioner to Kenya, Mr. Edward Clay, who gave the keynote address and our chief guest speaker, the Minister for Planning & National Development in Kenya, Prof. Anyang' Nyong'o. Participants were thrilled by the speakers' presentations. The participation was beyond our expectations and the feedback we have received so far has been very encouraging. We are already planning our next event–to keep the fires burning.

LESSONS LEARNED

This was a memorable experience for me. I experienced the power of teamwork, the power of partnership and the power of the individual in me. I feel complete, having achieved part of the British Council mission statement–creating opportunity for people in Mombasa and the world. The plan of action developed at the end of the Convention was in itself revealing. The participants called for more such events, sector specific events, and more importantly, they called for those who were not members to join the British Council Management Centre and the Management Forum.

As I said before, I love challenges–this left me a happy individual who had learned a lot along the way. I have developed my listening skills, intelligence research skills and analytical skills. I know that I need to keep providing services that add value to our partnership and in turn must challenge our partners to do the same so that we will have a valued and mutually beneficial partnership.

Through my experience starting the Management Forum in Mombasa, and my ongoing involvement with it, I have learned that to produce an excellent product like the Forum and the Convention, I need to understand both the business I am in and to understand people dynamics. This includes knowing my target audience, finding the right people to talk to, and developing relationships with them. In addition, I need to understand the market and to have good market judgement. I know now that this takes intuitive sense and feel, experience, and a certain way of thinking. I need to truly understand what my clients' needs are. I must have good client relationships so they will tell me their real concerns and needs so I will focus my efforts more appropriately. I must understand, too, the businesses they are in to be able to better define the benefits of the services I provide. I also learned that I need to design the right products and services to deliver to them.

This experience has helped me understand the dynamics of both designing and leading a team and an organization. The partnership with the Forum has given me an opportunity to think about the relationships of teams and organizations with their collaborators and communities, both locally and globally. It has also been a stimulating and mentally engaging experience that has broadened my thinking. The high caliber, smart, and industrious managers I have met and worked with have made my experience very rich and memorable. If you are looking to be challenged to think as a leader, as a manager and as a person, the Management Forum will not disappoint you.

Research Translation in South Africa

Mariam Stuurman

SUMMARY. It is estimated that 5 million South African adults and children are currently living with HIV/AIDS and because the scientific consensus is that an AIDS vaccine is the only way of curbing this pandemic, the South African HIV Vaccine Action Campaign (SA HIVAC) was established in 2000 as a community mobilisation and preparedness campaign to inform and educate the South African population about the HIV/AIDS vaccine development process. SA HIVAC includes an Information Clearinghouse whose role is to create an information system providing for the collection, storage and retrieval of information with the necessary architecture. This article describes the Information Clearinghouse's activities. *[Article copies available for a fee from The Haworth Document Delivery Service: 1-800-HAWORTH. E-mail address: <docdelivery@haworth press.com> Website: <http://www.HaworthPress.com> © 2002 by The Haworth Press, Inc. All rights reserved.]*

KEYWORDS. Research translation, knowledge translation, community mobilisation, HIV vaccines, Information Clearinghouse

According to the Joint United Nations Programme on HIV/AIDS (UNAIDS), HIV/AIDS is the number one cause of death in Africa. South Africa's AIDS epidemic is still the fastest growing in the world; it

---

Mariam Stuurman, ND, is Information Specialist, Library and Information Services, SA HIVAC (E-mail: mariam.stuurman@mrc.ac.za).

[Haworth co-indexing entry note]: "Research Translation in South Africa." Stuurman, Mariam. Co-published simultaneously in *Science & Technology Libraries* (The Haworth Information Press, an imprint of The Haworth Press, Inc.) Vol. 23, No. 2/3, 2002, pp. 145-150; and: *Leadership and Management Principles in Libraries in Developing Countries* (ed: Wei Wei, Sue O'Neill Johnson, and Sylvia E. A. Piggott) The Haworth Information Press, an imprint of The Haworth Press, Inc., 2002, pp. 145-150. Single or multiple copies of this article are available for a fee from The Haworth Document Delivery Service [1-800-HAWORTH, 9:00 a.m. - 5:00 p.m. (EST). E-mail address: docdelivery@haworthpress.com].

http://www.haworthpress.com/web/STL
© 2002 by The Haworth Press, Inc. All rights reserved.
Digital Object Identifier: 10.1300/J122v23n02_18

is estimated that roughly 5 million South African adults and children are currently living with HIV/AIDS. The scientific consensus is that an AIDS vaccine is the only way of curbing this pandemic. Historically, infectious diseases like smallpox, measles and yellow fever have been eradicated only by vaccines.[1]

The South African HIV Vaccine Action Campaign (SA HIVAC) was established in 2000 as a community mobilisation, education, information and human rights promotion campaign to inform and educate the South African population about HIV/AIDS vaccine development and clinical trials. The overall aim of the project is to create an enabling environment for full participation by communities in the process of HIV vaccine development and research. The project is a consortium consisting of individuals from various organisations and involving different skills including researchers (scientists); a legal staff (for human and legal rights issues); an ethics group researching current standards and a community mobilisation group that collaborates with different structures and community organisations.

The SA HIVAC project involves research translation. It relies heavily on communication strategies and knowledge management principles for effectiveness and/or success. 'Research translation' is an adaptation of a term first conceived by the Canadian Institutes of Health (CIHR). For the CIHR, knowledge translation is "the process of supporting the uptake of health research in a manner that improves the health and health care of a population through improved understandings, processes, services, products or systems." In this paper "research translation" takes a step beyond the knowledge management cycle; it is the exchange, synthesis and application to effect behavioral change.

Research is almost always academic, recorded only in academic literature and written in dense and specialised language. Very often, the benefits of this research are lost to the end-user as the target audience is not always the end-user, particularly in Africa where the Internet and technological access are scarce and problematic. Through research translation, we hope to create a society not only able to make, in this case, informed decisions about participation in vaccine trials, but also ongoing "behavioral change" choices.

THE INFORMATION CLEARINGHOUSE

While such goals are ambitious, an Information Clearinghouse has been established to achieve the following:

- A well-functioning information system integrating knowledge sources necessary for the optimal functioning of the project activities.
- An information resource accessible electronically by constituencies ranging from school children to policy makers.
- Specific information products and services for education and advocacy.
- A knowledge management system providing decision-support information.

The Information Clearinghouse was established in 2000 with the objective to create an information system providing for the collection, storage and retrieval of information with necessary architecture. The two main target groups/audiences are the staff involved in the vaccine initiative and the broader South African public. The Clearinghouse has a staff of four, including an information specialist, an editor, a journalist and a clinician.

The Clearinghouse includes an information management component as well as a media and communications component.

The information management component offers the following services:

- A reference service: sourcing, repackaging and document delivery of information to SA HIVAC staff as well as the staff of the different consortium members.
- A resource center open to the general public focusing not only on vaccine information, but general HIV information as well.
- Data collection from researchers for translation to "lay-speak."
- Background information provision for the development of media and information products. To date, a poster, brochure, training manual, comic book and facilitator's guide have been published.
- SDI services to the various consortium members on a monthly basis.
- Website maintenance: updating the information on www.saavi.org.za and www.afroaidsinfo.org. The development of a separate domain, www.sahivac.org.za, is currently underway.
- Specific vaccine candidate information at clinical trial sites.

The media and communications component is responsible for the collection of international and local media materials on HIV vaccines as well as the development of communication strategies and marketing/information products.

As illustrated above, the Clearinghouse has three foci; namely:

- Communicating the progress of vaccine development to various stakeholders and the South African public.
- Collecting comments from the public for identification of information needs and gaps to inform researchers as to the modification of current interventions.
- Recording the activities of the group for contribution to an international knowledge base.

The last is especially important as communities have never before been involved in vaccine development to this extent and these interventions are novel and innovative.

The ultimate outcome of this project is expected to be an improvement in individuals' knowledge to comprehend the complexities of HIV vaccine clinical trials and to make informed decisions in this regard. The following are seen as main indicators of success:

- Improved knowledge and understanding about HIV vaccines and trial participants' rights by the population within the three sites intended for vaccine clinical trials; in particular all trial participants and their families.
- Clinical trials in progress–ethics committees will not approve clinical trials until *informed* consent have been signed by all participants.
- Improved knowledge and understanding within civil society and at government level–demonstrated by survey outcome, laws and the number of paralegal services available.
- Participation of communities in debates, as well as extensive and ongoing media coverage–self-sustainable lobbying and/or advocacy drive.
- Number of requests for further information.

Baseline qualitative assessments were done at the beginning of the project and quantitative assessments have been continuous. Structured interviewer-administered questionnaires have been designed and used; the results are analysed by a clinical psychologist and a biostatistician.

Internal reviews are done on a monthly basis. The Information Clearinghouse is also subjected to external review by the main funders, namely the South African AIDS Vaccine Initiative (SAAVI) and the European Commission. Annual qualitative evaluations are done at selected intervention sites to determine knowledge and attitude changes, as well as shifts in comparison to baseline data.

LESSONS LEARNED

To date, the SA HIVAC project has been able to influence certain policies. For example, the long-term insurance industry has agreed to adapt their HIV testing protocol to accommodate clinical trial participants. Journal and news articles average 3 per month nationally. The South African government has pledged their support and funding to the vaccine initiative over the next 5 years.

Three years of experience with the project have taught us a few things, good and bad. We have learned that communication is extremely important, measurements are necessary for the identification of gaps in our interventions and that culture, at least in South Africa, plays an important role in the receptivity of our information and therefore indigenous knowledge systems should not be ignored. These are further discussed below.

Effective communication techniques and strategies are imperative to the success of this project. We started out with too many target groups (the general South African population) and have now narrowed it down to change agents representative of different targeted sectors within civil society. For different groups, it is also vital to use different techniques, e.g., scientists prefer electronic communications whereas the legal team prefer face-to-face interactions.

We have been very strict in analyzing the results of our questionnaires and surveys sent out. One of the gaps we've identified is the fact that language is a barrier. Many scientific terms do not even exist in the traditional African languages, so when translating our media products, we need to use a number of phrases and sentences to explain certain concepts. As a result, we have produced a comic book that describes the whole clinical trial process.

In certain ethnic communities, there is great mistrust about research and science. This stems from botched-up research trials in the past, not unlike the Tuskegee trials in America. During the Apartheid years, it has been said that biological warfare agents had been tested on political detainees and although it has never been proven, a large proportion of the population accept this as fact and have preconceived ideas regarding upcoming clinical trials. It is therefore imperative that we explain vaccine science in the context of indigenous knowledge systems. We need to start off with something communities can relate to–need to investigate what local communities know and have; and then illustrate how our "new" information can benefit them, not just as individuals but also as communities and ultimately, society. Indigenous knowledge is relevant for any development process and very often provides problem-solving strategies for local communities, especially the poor. It also represents an important contribution to global development knowledge which we should not lose sight of.

It is therefore important that we integrate indigenous knowledge systems more visibly and rigorously into our interventions. This would also prompt us to seek ways in which to codify indigenous knowledge so that it is never completely lost to the world. This process is important because indigenous knowledge is commonly held by communities and not by individuals. Therefore, in a region like Africa where communal life is still prominent, decisions and lifestyles are affected by indigenous knowledge.

In conclusion, this project proves that information and knowledge management forms an integral part of our lives but also assists in shaping our future. Very often, the information specialist is seen as a "support function." However, in this project, information management forms the centre and the basis of the project. It also highlights the communication skills often not visible in librarians or information professionals.

NOTE

1. UNAIDS. Report on the Global HIV/AIDS epidemic. Geneva: 2002.

EASTERN EUROPE

Working Locally, Thinking Globally in the Beginning of Library Management and Leadership

Toshka Borisova

SUMMARY. The paper provides an overview of the establishment and management of a special journalism library in Bulgaria thanks to the unique cooperation between Freedom Forum Foundation and American University in Bulgaria. It demonstrates one of the most distinctive characteristics of the AUBG Freedom Forum Journalism Library–the implemen-

Toshka Borisova is AUBG Freedom Forum Journalism Library Coordinator, American University in Bulgaria, Blagoevgrad, Bulgaria. She hold as a Master's degree in Bulgarian and Russian language and a Bachelor's degree in Library Science and Bibliography. She has 16 years of library experience and many publications in the Bulgarian specialized press (E-mail: Toshka@aubg.bg).

[Haworth co-indexing entry note]: "Working Locally, Thinking Globally in the Beginning of Library Management and Leadership." Borisova, Toshka. Co-published simultaneously in *Science & Technology Libraries* (The Haworth Information Press, an imprint of The Haworth Press, Inc.) Vol. 23, No. 2/3, 2002, pp. 151-160; and: *Leadership and Management Principles in Libraries in Developing Countries* (ed: Wei Wei, Sue O'Neill Johnson, and Sylvia E. A. Piggott) The Haworth Information Press, an imprint of The Haworth Press, Inc., 2002, pp. 153-160. Single or multiple copies of this article are available for a fee from The Haworth Document Delivery Service [1-800-HAWORTH, 9:00 a.m. - 5:00 p.m. (EST). E-mail address: docdelivery@haworthpress.com].

tation of innovations and new technologies. The library strives to meet the needs of patrons–students, professors and professional journalists promoting free press and speech in Bulgaria. *[Article copies available for a fee from The Haworth Document Delivery Service: 1-800-HAWORTH. E-mail address: <docdelivery@haworthpress.com> Website: <http://www.HaworthPress.com> © 2002 by The Haworth Press, Inc. All rights reserved.]*

KEYWORDS. Special library, management, journalism, e-services, cooperation, Bulgaria, Freedom Forum Foundation, innovation

The library community in Bulgaria is dynamic and constantly changing. Several major processes characterize the transformation of the Bulgarian library system during the transition period:

• Decentralization of the library system
• Abolition of ideological controls and censorship
• Restructuring the Library services and getting rid of old practices
• Introduction of Information technologies into library work and offering new formats of retrieval and dissemination of information
• Development of a national information resources market in a highly competitive environment.

How should one small library in Bulgaria position itself in the library network, so that it can meet the current and future challenges of the new time? What should constitute the measurement set to determine how effective it is as a leader among the special libraries in Bulgaria? These were the main focuses of my attention as a manager and researcher, and I will share my experience with you.

The AUBG Freedom Forum Journalism library in Bulgaria was created in 1992 as part of the international program of the American "Freedom Forum" foundation. The object of the program is to establish libraries dedicated to freedom of thought and expression in different parts of the world. One of the main goals of AUBG Freedom Forum Journalism Library is to serve as a model to all special libraries in Bulgaria, providing new information services and resources to its clientele, setting new practices and tendencies, applying the best library practices worldwide. I was inspired to do so using the rich American experience, and motivated by the thought that even the not well-known Bulgarian library practice could be innovative and could offer so many opportunities for that. I simply needed a good strategy that could force the development of the library as a powerful distributive channel for information, and change the role of a librarian turning him into mediator of information and knowledge manager. What were the steps?

- Defining adequate acquisition policy
- Promoting the library collections
- Offering modern form of custom-tailored services
- Training library users
- Providing access to information.

I thought of everything that could transform my library into a hosting place for sharing and creating story ideas; into a real center of knowledge, research, freedom and independence. To complete this transformation Freedom Forum Journalism Library needed a new management model that could implement the new concepts of diversity and pluralism of ideas. Library management as a whole is a complex issue. For a small special library it is even more complex. Especially, bearing in mind that AUBG Freedom Forum Journalism Library has a special statute, as follows:

- Library is located in an academic library as an independent body. The advantage of this is that it operates with more resources, other subject collections and databases that are beyond its subject coverage.
- Library is a product of the cooperation between AUBG in Bulgaria and the Freedom Forum Foundation. Freedom Forum Foundation, USA, financially supports the library. Library has its ten-year-old history–six years as a separate collection and four years under a librarian's management.
- The library is the only special library of journalism and mass communication in the region, and has the largest English language collection in this field. The collection is unique for Bulgaria, and Balkan countries.
- The Library is not situated in the capital, but has obligations to organize its activities not only locally, but also to act at a national level.

Library management is complicated, too. It is a living part of an academic library, and has to act as such. On the other hand, it has to conduct its own policy serving journalists from the region and promoting the Freedom Forum Foundation policy. Freedom Forum Library has relatively independent library management. The Librarian reports to the AUBG Library director and to the Freedom Forum Library Director in Arlington (see Figure 1).

FIGURE 1. Levels of Communication

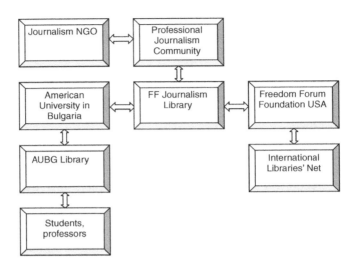

The primary goals of Library management are fostering the following library activities:

1. To determine the strategic intent,
2. To provide opportunities and environment to get results,
3. To bring innovations into practice.

DETERMINATION OF THE STRATEGIC INTENT

The mission of the Freedom Forum Library is to meet the educational needs of students and faculty at AUBG and to support their research, as well as to support Bulgarian journalists, offering them the information they need in all possible formats. That means the right information resource for the right users at the right time.

OPPORTUNITIES FOR RESULTS

This implies good management of library activities, communications and implementation of best practices. Special attention should be given to the three basic constituencies of the library–collection, services, and readers' profile. The librarian is a mediator between them. The librarian is the connection (see Figure 2).

FIGURE 2. Model of Interaction

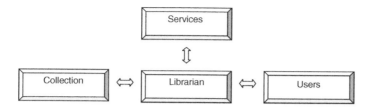

COLLECTIONS

Collections and specific holdings are the major factor attracting an audience to a specific library. AUBG Freedom Forum Library has two collections–one supported by Freedom Forum Foundation, and another one, the private collection of Leonard Marks–former chairman of USA Information Agency–a kindly donation to AUBG Library. The former is growing; the latter is constant. One of the permanent activities in the area of collection development is to observe collections, to compare their content with the courses taught at the AUBG, to evaluate the core collection and constantly select new titles of monographs and information resources to further improve the existing collections. This task is further complicated by the fact that providing resources for professionals contradicts the collection development policy of AUBG Library, which is focused only on the English language library materials, as AUBG is an English-language community.

Collection development is a long and highly responsible process. Academic curriculum is dynamic, and its content and priorities are changing constantly. Many visitors asked me lately why the collection was so pro American, and they said they needed a European oriented journalism collection. Some have found only a few books on Internet Journalism. And others found that the library did not have resources on computer design. I noticed the growing interest in journalism in the countries in transition, and put this as a priority in the next year budgeting for collection development. A library collection is like a live body–it needs constant feeding and attention.

SERVICES

The link between library collections and the library users are the services provided. AUBG library has laid the groundwork for a modern public service, but many things are yet to be done and improved. Providing better user-oriented services is an important factor for all library activities. Both services marketing and services improvement are important for users' need assessment. If we ignore users' service needs, we will create the conflicts of expectations and will lose them. One of the first things to do while assuming my first work duties was to draw public attention to the library. As Freedom Forum Journalism Library was a department of a bigger library, there was not a managerial vision of how to do it at that time. A lot of potential users didn't know about the library and its holdings. And it was a good starting point for a promotional campaign. I used every single opportunity to catch the users' attention. I wrote an action plan that included activities oriented to the targeted library audiences (journalists and academic community), and general public, as a whole. The academic community was activated via different methods and strategies I used. I gave them presentations on services we provide; taught them how to improve their information skills, gave a few bibliographic instruction lectures; provided reference services, offered both on-line and on-site, I published posters and leaflets, subject bibliographies, and organized seminars, special events and lectures from special guests, which, as a whole made the Freedom Forum Journalism Library their favorite place in the library, but, aside from that, developed their professional interests, turned them into life-long learners, improved their information skills, and supported their study as a whole.

Other outreach activities focused on local journalists. To make sure they felt comfortable in the library, I designed and taught classes as part of their continuing education, such as: Internet for Journalists, How to Search Information on Internet, and organized a seminar "How to write news."

An important accent of my work was on cooperation. This turned out to be a winning card for a small library. We contacted local media organizations–Local Unit of Union of Bulgarian Journalists-Blagoevgrad, and worked closely with them; we found support and cooperation with organizations at a national level. The library became a partner with the Bulgarian Media Coalition–the biggest journalism organization in Bulgaria in organizing a national conference about NGOs in media. The library is a resource center to Bulgarian Media Coalition and the program "Access to information."

To reach the general audience in the region I participated in a few radio shows, talking about the principles of Freedom Forum Foundation, its libraries, our library in particular; promoted library resources and activities; published a series of articles; participated in conferences, etc.

Creation of a web site and E-reference services was oriented to everyone.

USERS

Audience segmentation is a considerable part and important focus of my managerial work planning services, responsive to specific user needs and their environment. And a close contact with users is substantial to exchange ideas, to get their reactions, and share different experiences. The library serves two main groups of users–academic community, and professional community. Each of the groups has its own specifics and peculiarities. The first group is constituted of faculty and students–again, the two subgroups have specifics that should be considered at all levels, designing services that will be adequate to their educational and research needs. I have to follow all programs and courses in the curricula, I have to individually meet each faculty, and get acquainted with their teaching methods and style of presenting materials, to support their work with the appropriate information resources. The second group–the one that includes professional journalists–turned out to be more unpredictable. I thought I had a vision of their expectations for the library resources, but working with them I found out that their low language proficiency and lack of good computer and information skills affected the proper use of the library resources.

INNOVATIONS

The third area that needed special managerial focus was the process of reshaping the services and implementation of innovative practices. Implementing something new, getting rid of stereotypes and historical practices, bringing to the attention of the public something unusual, something modern and close to their current needs and corresponding to their new skills and knowledge, improves the status of the library, and is a good way to attract a new public to it.

One of the initiatives of Freedom Forum Library is the challenge to create a Bibliography of Bulgarian Journalism. In the last ten years no Bulgarian libraries, nor any professional institution collected bibliographic records, or information in the area of journalism. As a librarian, I knew how heavily used were the two volumes of the bibliography "Bulgarian Journalism 1944-1969," Sofia: Research center of journalism, 1972; "Bulgarian Journalism 1970-1980," Sofia: Research center of journalism, 1985. This center had been closed a few years before. During my career I collected a lot of materials for journalism. And, at a certain point, I decided to prepare a selected bibliography for the last 11 years. It is a very interesting period from the Bulgarian media history, but what is most important, the new journalism generation needed information about the processes, and wanted to know what had happened. The bibliography is prepared to serve as a reference tool and to locate materials for further research and reading. At the moment, this bibliography is just a huge computer file, as funds for its publication, are scarce. Other bibliographies, published as leaflets in the FF Library are: Mass Media in Europe; Media and Elections; Media Law and Regulations; Public Relations Bibliography; Women and Media; Internet Journalism; Media and NGO, etc. These materials support the educational process at AUBG, thus the AUBG Freedom Forum Library becomes an active academic partner in the teaching-learning process.

This year, with the support and cooperation of the University Media Relations Office, I started another project, "AUBG in media." Practically, this is an attempt to put together and organize the representation of the institutional history through the prism of mass media coverage. The idea for this project, again, came from the heavy demand for materials for the institutional history.

I mentioned earlier about the design of AUBG Freedom Forum Library web site (accessible on http://www.aubg.bg/fforum) offering E-reference services (see Figure 3). E-reference is an add-one service and it increased the number of visitors. This is still not a library practice in Bulgaria, and is relatively new to our audience. This project, like all other initiatives of the Freedom Forum library, is driven by consumer demand. AUBG students and faculty warmly welcomed the services, and started to use it heavily. Very soon, we started to receive requests for information from Germany, Turkey, France, and other countries in Europe. Within three working days the librarian performs the necessary queries and prepares a list of resources. In two years I received over 400 references. The web site is not designed by a professional. I worked on its design and content. The page has two versions–in English and in Bulgarian. I am happy that it had been noticed by Bulgarian librarians, and was awarded first place in the Bulgarian Librarian competition for the best web site.

What distinguishes Freedom Forum Library is that it offers more and more information resources in electronic formats. As AUBG Library has subscribed and provides access to the most renowned information aggregators–*EBSCO*, *JSTOR*, *ProQuest*, encyclopedias and other reference resources in electronic formats; Freedom Forum Journalism Library offers access to a wide range of modern electronic resources. On the other hand, through the subscription of *NYT*, *WP*, *WSJ*, *USA Today* on CD-ROM, AUBG Library enriches its collections. AUBG On-Line catalogue (http://oralin.aubg.bg) is accessible around

FIGURE 3. Example Screenshot from AUBG Freedom Forum Journalism Library

the clock, thus all journalistic resources are available to the public almost around the clock.

At last, working locally and thinking globally is not only a slogan. AUBG Freedom Forum Journalism Library in Bulgaria established itself as an innovative research and educational center.

Librarianship in Azerbaijan: What Can a Leader Do?

Muzhgan Nazarova

SUMMARY. To be successful library leaders in the 21st century, it is important to make decisions that blend the strengths of the past, the demands of the present, and the uncertainty of the future as well as to have someone who will take a lead. Emotional intelligence (EI) is a crucial component of leadership. The five components of EI are examined in the article. Based on a testimony of a librarian from Azerbaijan, who envisioned the changes taking place in the profession and became a catalyst of these changes, the article describes a development of Azerbaijani librarianship for the last 10 years. *[Article copies available for a fee from The Haworth Document Delivery Service: 1-800-HAWORTH. E-mail address: <docdelivery@haworthpress.com> Website: <http://www.HaworthPress.com> © 2002 by The Haworth Press, Inc. All rights reserved.]*

KEYWORDS. Azerbaijan, leader, leadership, librarianship, special librarianship, libraries

My career in special librarianship started in 1982, when I was hired by the Republican Medical Research Library of Azerbaijan, in Baku. At that

Muzhgan Nazarova is Founder, Azerbaijani Library Development Association and PhD student, Graduate School of Library and Information Science (GSLIS), University of Illinois at Urbana-Champaign (E-mail: nazarova@students.uiuc.edu).

[Haworth co-indexing entry note]: "Librarianship in Azerbaijan: What Can a Leader Do?" Nazarova, Muzhgan. Co-published simultaneously in *Science & Technology Libraries* (The Haworth Information Press, an imprint of The Haworth Press, Inc.) Vol. 23, No. 2/3, 2002, pp. 161-169; and: *Leadership and Management Principles in Libraries in Developing Countries* (ed: Wei Wei, Sue O'Neill Johnson, and Sylvia E. A. Piggott) The Haworth Information Press, an imprint of The Haworth Press, Inc., 2002, pp. 161-169. Single or multiple copies of this article are available for a fee from The Haworth Document Delivery Service [1-800-HAWORTH, 9:00 a.m. - 5:00 p.m. (EST). E-mail address: docdelivery@haworthpress.com].

time, I did not realize I was destined to become a catalyst for change in the field. This first occurred to me eleven years later while I was mastering the principles of leadership and management in a Certificate in Management Studies Program at a Business School at Nottingham Trent University. While studying different leadership theories and comparing them with the leadership experiences that I had in high school and college, I realized that I had certain skills and abilities that would help me to advance in my career and make significant changes in the profession. As soon as I received my Certificate in Management in September 1993, I was hired by the United States Information Agency (USIA) as director of the Information Resource Center (IRC) in Baku, Azerbaijan. It was my first administrative job. I started as a solo librarian and ended up supervising four people by the end of my first year. Though I envisioned the changes that could be done in my work, I did not suspect that my vision would help to bring about such drastic changes in the profession in my country. Once engaged as a leader, I started to make things happen not only at my workplace but also far beyond it. How did this happen? Was I born as a leader or made? How did I learn leadership? Who helped me learn? Why does my leadership matter?

AZERBAIJAN

I am from Azerbaijan, one of the countries of the Former Soviet Union, located at the crossroads of Europe, Asia and the Middle East. Azerbaijan was founded in 1918, then joined the Soviet Union and remained a part of it until it gained its independence in 1991. Since 1994, Azerbaijan has become well known all over the world for its oil and energy reserves, and has entered into partnerships with the world's leading oil companies. The history of libraries in this country goes back to the thirteenth century when the first library, holding more than 400,000 volumes, was founded by Nasreddin Tusi, a great thinker and scientist of the period (Nazarova 1998). There are approximately 10,000 libraries in Azerbaijan today, and 30,000 professional librarians and technical staff work in them. Librarianship is considered mostly a female occupation and women usually hold the top administrative positions. The library administrators were trained during Soviet times and their management and leadership style has not changed. To continue being successful library leaders in the 21st century, they will need to make decisions that blend strengths of the past, the demands of the present, and the uncertainty of the future (Metz 2001). They will need to develop, strengthen and exercise their leadership skills to be better equipped to meet the challenges they will face to bring the libraries into the new century. In order for this process to start someone had to take the lead.

Library and information professionals in special library services in developed countries are facing the following three major paradigm shifts (Marshall et al., 1996):

- Transition from paper to electronic media as the dominant form of information storage and retrieval;
- Increasing demand for accountability, including a focus on customers, performance measurement, benchmarking and continuous improvement;
- New forms of work organization, including end-user computing, job-sharing, telework, etc.

At the same time their colleagues in Azerbaijan–a developing country– are facing completely different challenges:

- Very limited funds for collection development and collections that consist mostly of print media;
- Absolute lack of technological developments in libraries;
- Inability to meet the information needs of their customers due to a lack of proper resources;
- Limited knowledge about advancements in the field, including electronic media.

This list can go on and on but it quickly becomes obvious that the rapid economic development of this oil-rich country in this era of globalization has not been matched by developments in special librarianship. Advances in librarianship can be a real asset and play a critical role in the country's development by providing information to the organizations and people who move the country forward. However, someone has to take a leadership role and start making things happen.

LEADERS ARE NOT BORN, THEY ARE MADE

Before I studied management and leadership theories I did not realize that certain skills and abilities–like self-confidence, self-assessment, optimism, a strong drive to achieve, persuasiveness, and the ability to lead teams–I was given by nature, are the components of emotional intelligence (Goleman 2001). Emotional intelligence is a crucial component of leadership and those who have it make the most effective leaders. Goleman (2001) provides definition and hallmarks of the following five components of emotional intelligence at work: self-awareness, self-regulation, motivation, empathy and social skill. Self-awareness is the ability to recognize and understand your moods, emotions, and drives, as well as their effect on others. Self-confidence, realistic self-assessment, and a self-deprecating sense of humor are the hallmarks of self-awareness. A second component is self-regulation, which is defined as the ability to control or redirect disruptive impulses and moods; the propensity to suspend judgment–to think before acting with trustworthiness and integrity, comfort with ambiguity, and openness to change being its hallmarks. A third component of emotional intelligence is motivation which means a passion to work for reasons that go beyond money or status and a propensity to pursue goals with energy and persistence and having a strong drive to achieve optimism and organizational commitment as its hallmarks. Empathy as the ability to understand the emotional makeup of other people and the skill in treating people according to their emotional reactions is named as the fourth component. Expertise in building and retaining this talent, cross-cultural sensitivity, and service to clients and customers are described as its hallmarks. The last component is social skill defined as a proficiency in managing relationships and building networks and an ability to find common ground and build rapport. Effectiveness in leading change, persuasiveness, and expertise in building and leading teams are described as the hallmarks of social skill (Goleman 2001).

The components of emotional intelligence indicate a great potential to become a leader. But again, having potential does not guarantee that you will become one. Emotional intelligence is only one element of all the necessary components of a successful leader. In addition to having the necessary skills, abilities and knowledge, one also needs a deep understanding of leadership and needs to have a kind of passion about it.

> To understand leadership, one must understand its essential nature–that is, the process of the leader and followers engaging in reciprocal influence to achieve a shared purpose. Leadership is all about getting people to work together to make things happen that might not otherwise occur or prevent things from happening that would ordinarily take place. (Rosenbach and Taylor 2001, 1)

One cannot make an effective leader without having a vision.

But there is something more, in addition to all the above-mentioned elements that really make a successful leader. Based on my personal experience, it includes the role models that you meet throughout your career, as well as the organization that you work in and the conditions, both professional and social, that you function in. Getting to know, working with and being mentored by the distinguished leaders in the field helps you to mobilize all the potential and abilities you have to become like them and make a difference in your professional world. This is a real challenge. But that is what makes a real leader. These sorts of experiences influenced my becoming a leader.

WHAT MAKES A GOOD LEADER?

Based on Gardner (1990) and Prime (1995), John Berry (1998) provides the following characteristics of leadership:

> True leadership respects no boundaries. Leaders liberate both themselves and those around them. They tear down walls; they see the bigger picture, the longer term. They reach outside and beyond their turf and constituencies. They "rise above their jurisdiction." They see and understand the relationship of their enterprise to the rest of the community, world, and universe. Leaders risk making decisions on a case-by-case basis, not by a rulebook or policy manual.

In order to be able to execute these leadership actions, one needs to be in the appropriate circumstances and environment. The library administrators in Azerbaijan who have been used to the Soviet style of leadership and administration and needed to develop their leadership skills to meet the challenges of the new century, for example, do not fit J. Berry's description of leaders. Even though they realize the existing needs and see the bigger picture, they still don't know how to liberate themselves and their colleagues to reach outside and make things happen. In my opinion, they might have been able to experience that liberation if they were functioning in a different social and cultural environment. One has to be in the right place at the right time. Sometimes it takes only one person, one with the right vision who understands the situation and is ready to reorganize, revise, rebuild and transform everything surrounding them, and then empower the people around them to follow their example.

My Testimony

None of the theories of leadership that I became acquainted with mention the element of "being a first" as an important factor for success. Maybe because I was the first citizen of a country of eight million to take certain steps in a professional career, I felt responsibe to advance the profession and lead its progress. When I started to work at the IRC at the United States Information Service (USIS) in Baku in 1993 not a single other library in the country had a computer. Librarians would come and visit the IRC as if it were a museum full of artifacts that they had never seen in their lives. At that time I thought about how it would be possible to transfer this model to other libraries in the country. However, I was still in the process of learning about new things myself. I was entering the world of American librarianship and everything was absolutely new to me. While USIA libraries/information centers had existed in many parts of the world for a long time, my task was to start a library from scratch in Baku and base it on the models used in other developing countries. It was a challenging but pleasant task. It took me a while to get the IRC up and running. My main responsibility was to provide high quality service to the U.S. Embassy personnel, Americans and other foreigners doing business and working in Azerbaijan, as well as to the local community. Since the Embassy people were expecting service equal to what they would be getting at home, I had to keep up in terms of professional development and gain the necessary skills and abilities to provide adequate service. At the same time, I had to serve the local audience, which did not have any previous exposure to the kind of resources that I had and the services that I was providing. I was also trying to share my experiences at my job with other library professionals in my country. In the meantime, I started a number of interesting initiatives at work, which included different kinds of outreach as well as special services on demand. For example, back in 1993, nobody knew about e-reference. Since Embassy officials were busy with their other tasks, we developed a system of placing their requests electronically, which we then answered in a timely manner. The different innovative ideas that I came up with completely changed the role of the IRC not only in the Embassy but also in the community as a whole.

In 1994, I was sent to the U.S. for training. I attended the American Library Association (ALA) Conference in Miami as part of the program. It was there, in Miami, that ALA entered my life. That conference gave me an opportunity to seriously think about the libraries and librarians of my country. I knew then that this was to be my mission and that I would be able to make a difference in Azerbaijan. Upon returning home I realized that without a professional degree in library science, I would not be able to accomplish a lot. I became the first Azerbaijani librarian to get an MLS from an American library school. During my two years at graduate school I was blessed to be around real experts, professionals and leaders. As I mentioned above, I happened to in the right place at the right time. I started to attend ALA conferences, got to know people, and made some presentations. I was proud that I was representing my country, even though not much was being accomplished there. I realized that only by having a strong library association can we move the libraries of Azerbaijan forward and be able to speak about the important issues in librarianship. When I returned home I continued to work in the IRC in the Embassy and to use innovative approaches in my work. I knew then that a time of great change for the librarians of my country had arrived. In 1999, with the support and help of thousands of professionals in my country who believed in my vision, I founded the Azerbaijani Library Development Association (AzLA) (http://azla.aznet.org/azla/), the first professional association in my country. Ann Symons, the president of ALA, whom I met at one of the conferences, became my role model and mentor. After working with me for some time as my mentor, she visited Azerbaijan with two American colleagues and conducted a workshop for the librarians entitled: "Cooperation for library development: on library associations, consortia, and other collaborative approaches." Detailed information about the workshop as well as the other activities of AzLA can be found at AzLA's websites: http://leep.lis.uiuc.edu/publish/Azerbaijani_ Library_Association/public_html/ azla_activities.html; http://azla.aznet.org/ azla/Cont_ALA/cont_ala.html. That workshop was the beginning of revolutionary changes in librarianship in Azerbaijan. It awakened hundreds of professionals who had been dealing with a lot of problems at their work because of the lack of financial support, proper equipment, and normal working conditions. Before, there had been no hope for the future of the Azerbaijani libraries. Through my efforts, AzLA became a leading force in developing the profession. I continued to share my vision with colleagues and to educate them about the opportunities that could change their lives. It is amazing to see all the accomplishments of the Azerbaijani libraries in the short time period since 1999. My vision of library development went even beyond my country. Now the librarians of Azerbaijan are working together with their colleagues from Armenia and Georgia with the help of the ALA.

Detailed information about the cooperation in South Caucasus can be found at a website of the ALA's International Relations Committee on the Caucasus: http://www.ala.org/Content/NavigationMenu/Our_Association/ Offices/International_Relations2/Activities_and_Projects/Strengthening_ Library_Association.htm. A power point presentation created by one of the American participants of the workshop–Sylva Natalie Manoogian is a virtual demonstration of the workshop: http://leep.lis.uiuc.edu/seworkspace/ nazarova/Tbilisi/Tbilisi/index.htm.

Today, the librarians of Azerbaijan are thinking about how to increase the number of Internet public access terminals in their libraries and how to get subscriptions to different online databases. They now have access to EBSCO. They are familiar with the Library of Congress and Dewey Decimal classification systems, have a clear idea about MARC and Dublin Core and are talking about which library automation system to choose. Most librarians have e-mail accounts and some of them use the IRC and messenger services to communicate with their colleagues overseas. They dream about digitizing their library collections.

It is impossible to talk about all the dramatic changes that occurred in the profession over such a short time. There is still a long way for Azerbaijani libraries to go. But the journey has started and I feel that the future will be bright. I know that in this century we will need to train our professionals to meet all the technical, intellectual, and ethical challenges facing the profession today. My main goal now is to completely redesign library education in Azerbaijan, start a Library School based on the American model, and educate a new generation of information professionals in my country.

REFERENCES

Berry III, J. 1998. Leadership liberates. *Library Journal* 09 (15): 6.

Evan, St. L. 1998. Prime leadership. *Library Journal* 09 (15): 36-39.

Gardner, J.W. 1990. *On leadership*. New York: Free Press.

Goleman, D. 2001. "What makes a leader?" In *Contemporary issues in leadership*, ed. W. Rosenbach and R. Taylor. 5-18. Boulder, CO: Westview Press.

Marshall, J., B. Fisher, L. Moulton, and R. Piccolli. 1996. *Competencies for special librarians of the 21st century*. Submitted to the SLA Board of Directors by the Special Committee on Competencies for Special Librarians, May 1996. <http://www.sla.org/content/ SLA/professional/meaning/competency.cfm>.

Metz, T. 2001. Wanted: library leaders for a discontinuous future. *Library Issues* 21 (3): 1-6.

Nazarova, Muzhgan. 1998. "Libraries in Azerbaijan: Reaching forward." In *Libraries: Local touch–global reach*, ed. K. de la Pena McCook, B.Ford, and K. Lippincott, 82-89. Chicago and London: ALA.

Rosenbach, W., and R. Taylor, eds. 2001. *Contemporary issues in leadership*. 5th ed. Boulder, CO: Westview Press.

CENTRAL AMERICA

Cautious but Decisive:
Ten Years of Information Services
Implementation at the Universidad
Francisco Marroquín in Guatemala

Grete Pasch

SUMMARY. The Universidad Francisco Marroquín (UFM), a private university, was founded in Guatemala City in 1971. UFM follows a "cautious but decisive" strategy for information services development: a promising and potentially disruptive technology is researched and experimented with on a small scale before campus-wide adoption. The library has provided an ideal testing ground for Ethernet wiring, wireless access, CD-ROMs, multimedia, Internet, and web-based application development. In addition, two spinoff projects have blossomed: UFM's integrated library

Grete Pasch, MLIS, MSc, BSc, is Director, New Media/Recursos Digitales, Universidad Francisco Marroquin, 6 Calle Final Zona 10, Guatemala City, Guatemala (E-mail: gpasch@ufm.edu.gt. URL: www.newmedia.ufm.edu.gt).

[Haworth co-indexing entry note]: "Cautious but Decisive: Ten Years of Information Services Implementation at the Universidad Francisco Marroquín in Guatemala." Pasch, Grete. Co-published simultaneously in *Science & Technology Libraries* (The Haworth Information Press, an imprint of The Haworth Press, Inc.) Vol. 23, No. 2/3, 2002, pp. 171-179; and: *Leadership and Management Principles in Libraries in Developing Countries* (ed: Wei Wei, Sue O'Neill Johnson, and Sylvia E. A. Piggott) The Haworth Information Press, an imprint of The Haworth Press, Inc., 2002, pp. 171-179. Single or multiple copies of this article are available for a fee from The Haworth Document Delivery Service [1-800-HAWORTH, 9:00 a.m. - 5:00 p.m. (EST). E-mail address: docdelivery@haworthpress.com].

system is supplied by glifos.com to regional libraries, and the New Media department works with indexed streaming video for web-based learning and local resource archiving. *[Article copies available for a fee from The Haworth Document Delivery Service: 1-800-HAWORTH. E-mail address: <docdelivery@ haworthpress.com> Website: <http://www.HaworthPress.com> © 2002 by The Haworth Press, Inc. All rights reserved.]*

KEYWORDS. Information technology, library services, integrated library system, innovation, rich media, streaming video, disruptive technologies

INTRODUCTION

The Universidad Francisco Marroquín (UFM) is a private university that was founded in Guatemala City in 1971. Current enrollment is 2,500 full time students. Degrees are granted in business administration (undergraduate and MBA programs), economics, law, political science, architecture, social sciences, education, medicine, and dentistry.

In 1988 the UFM moved to a new campus. Built among wooded hills, it is isolated from the hustle and bustle of the big city and offers a beautiful setting for reflection and study. Once settled on the new campus, the UFM administration started planning the creation of adequate information services.

Given that resources are limited, the strategy adopted for information services investment has been "cautious but decisive." This works as follows: a technology or service is researched, tried on a small scale, experimented with, and if results are encouraging, adopted campus-wide. This was how the network infrastructure was built, how the library systems blossomed, and how work is proceeding on an archive of educational resources that concentrates heavily on digital video and its uses for supporting the UFM's educational mission.

BUILDING AN IT INFRASTRUCTURE

The Library: A Key Player in Technology Innovation

Since the UFM was founded, the library has played a crucial role in supporting the University's educational mission and in testing and introducing key technologies. The library occupies a 3,500m² building that by mid-2003 housed 80,000 volumes and over 800 periodical titles, plus a collection of video tapes, and rare books and maps. It is one of only a handful of libraries in the country that offer open-shelf access to any person (UFM member or not) who wishes to use the collection. This building was the first one on campus, and in 1993 one of the first in Guatemala, to be wired with Cat5 cabling. Other firsts included CD-ROM stations for database searching, a touchscreen station for user information, and a home-grown barcode controlled system for photocopy self-service that is in use since 1993.

The integrated library system is a good example of cautious but decisive innovation. Instead of importing an expensive system, the decision was made to design and implement such software locally (Pasch & Arias, 1995). Fundraising by the Friends of the Library Group and donations in kind by Sun Microsystems and Informix Inc. ensured the needed financial and technical resources. The first version of the system, called "Infolib," was launched in 1993. It was so successful, that it has been further developed into a commercial product called "GLIFOS," a fully web-enabled and XML-based application marketed by glifos.com. Over 40 libraries in Guatemala, El Salvador, Honduras, Panamá, and México have chosen "GLIFOS" over other library applications. One of the key features of Glifos is that it allows for copy cataloging from potentially any other web-based library catalog, using Dublin Core, MARC, or any other parseable webpage structure. GLIFOS imports all recognized controlled fields and automatically translates their contents from other languages into Spanish for faster inclusion into local catalogs.

Building a Campus Wide IT Infrastructure

In 1996, universities were among the first Guatemalan institutions that benefitted from government approval to connect to the Internet. The project that made this possible was the Organization of American States–sponsored "Mayapaq" network (Pasch & Valdés, 1996). The UFM's board of directors had first discussed the Internet's possibilities in 1993. As a result, the first campus fiber-optic connections were approved and installed starting in 1995, under the supervision of Dr. Rafael Mendía. Finally, on October 9, 1996, Mr. Juan Carlos López was hired to manage the first 64Kbps Internet connection to the UFM campus. This *Centro de Operaciones de Internet* (COI)–that is, the Internet Operations Center–was housed in the library building, and remains there to this day, although its functions have expanded significantly. The COI manages all IT infrastructure projects at the UFM. All buildings have been wired and interconnected via fiber-optic lines, bringing email access to all. Today, the campus uses four E1 lines for Internet and network-based phone services. Wireless access covers most public and teaching areas. Computer labs offer over 250 machines for student use, staff uses an additional 150. The University funds a two-year credit line for all students and faculty who wish to buy their own laptops.

The COI is still run by Juan Carlos López and his team of 3 FTEs, who obviously have their hands full 24/7. Current IT projects include installing audiovisual equipment, such as ceiling-mounted projectors, screens, and speakers in all classrooms. They also manage the UFM website and its associated teaching portal, which are used by UFM professors as well as several local high schools–thus the need for 32 adequately firewalled servers.

ENTERING THE NEW MEDIA ERA

The Temptation of eLearning

In 1997, Clayton Christensen published "The Innovator's Dilemma," where he introduced the concept of disruptive vs. sustaining technologies. Disruptive technologies, says Christensen, are those that bring a significant change in common practice, but that do so in a way that is not immediately noticed by the mainstream. These technologies are typically smaller or cheaper or more convenient, but they underperform the established products (Christensen, 1997).

What is disturbing about disruptive technologies is that they create new markets, which expand until the established markets are destroyed. Graduate schools of management, and classroom and campus-based instruction are seen by Christensen as established technologies for teaching, while corporate universities and "distance education, typically enabled by the Internet," are potentially disruptive technologies (p. xxv).

By the late 1990s, the UFM enjoyed the IT infrastructure and the level of user expertise that would have been fertile ground for the fiery eLearning enthusiasm that was sweeping the higher education community. Universities were funding huge programs for creating and offering eLearning or web-based distance education. Most of these efforts failed miserably (Hafner, 2002), with the latest casualty being fathom.com, an online provider of courses for self-directed learners. In an email to registered members (dated February 26, 2003), the Fathom consortium announced it would be closing by the end of March, 2003–that is, less than three years after it was launched with much expectation by a consortium of fourteen highly respected institutions that included Columbia University, the London School of Economics, the British Library, and the University of Chicago. Other endeavors that were succeeding, such as the University of Phoenix, required a large upfront investment in marketing and support.

What saved the UFM from following this risky path was the "cautious" approach. During the year 2000, it was decided that dedicating resources to offer online degrees was not advised, since there was no way to test the feasibility of such endeavors on a small scale. But the challenge of the Internet to education was clear, and the UFM needed to start building the necessary expertise. Innovative as the library had been, it did not have the capability or the culture to experiment with such educational technologies, while the COI's mission remained one of maintaining the IT infrastructure. Giancarlo Ibárgüen, the Secretary General of the UFM, applied one of the key ideas for managing disruptive technologies: spinning off an independent group to experiment with the application of new technologies for Internet enabling teaching (Christensen, p. 217). Thus was born the New Media department.

New Media at the UFM

This author accepted the challenge of creating the new New Media department. In early 2001, the mission statement for New Media read: "to assist faculty members, researchers, and students in the use, creation, and management of digital resources that complement their academic work." What would this entail at the practical level? MartinWeller, senior lecturer at Open University, argues that if the Internet is used as a sustaining technology in education, it will fail to be all it can be (Weller, 2001). New Media could start by digitizing documents, creating websites, and opening chatrooms to support online courses. But it was known from previous experiences (Pasch & Stewart, 2002) that there was a better way to deliver course materials: streaming video.

The idea is simple. Instead of writing texts that become the central content of a course, a lecturer would be videotaped in his own environment, doing what he does best: teaching in a classroom, interacting with students. Then the video would be edited, indexed, and posted online. Two objectives would be fulfilled: the video would serve as material for potential online courses, and the effort would help preserve the best that the UFM has to offer, namely, the teaching value of local Faculty members.

To achieve a technically superior product on a reasonable budget, the production equipment was carefully selected (two miniDV cameras,

Premiere 6 and Vegas Video 3 software, free tools from Real Networks and Microsoft to deliver streaming video) and the idea was tested. The first step consisted of recording, editing, and indexing several independent lectures. Then, during the Fall of 2001, a full semester course was taped. This course, an introduction to everyday logic, was taught by Armando de la Torre, one of UFM's most esteemed professors.

From January to May 2002, the first group of 30 students took this course online, using the indexed videos as the main course materials. Full technical support was provided, both online and during face to face sessions with the professor. The web-based group was compared to a second group of 30 students who studied the same contents, but in a traditional classroom setting. Both groups had similar learning styles, IQ, and personality traits. Grades showed no significant differences. At the end of the semester, the video-based group showed a higher level of satisfaction with the course, while the classroom group still was very skeptical about the possibility of online learning.

The video-based group was especially pleased that they were more in control of the class. They could pause and replay the video as often as they wanted. They could choose not to watch the video on a particular day. They could skip ahead and check out future lectures. They could listen and watch or just listen. They could watch the video individually or in a group. In the words of Jonathan Levy, vice-president at Harvard Business Online, "disintermediation means the student is driving" (Levy, 2001), an effect that some educators would certainly find "disruptive."

The cautious approach worked once again. A practical way had been found to create online materials that could be used to create courses and that were also valuable reference sources. Since then, four additional video-based, full semester courses are in use. Dozens of conferences have been built by applying the same production principles. The next step was to decisively adopt and expand this concept, which is being achieved by following the technical strategies described next.

Rich Media Strategies

Glifos.com developed for us a video player that combines video with a video index, transcriptions, references to websites, windows for notes, credits, images such as powerpoint slides, and almost any other material that one could think of to enrich the video experience (see Figure 1).

The technical strategies being applied include:

- Everything that is integrated into the player is described in XML, thus creating platform independent metadata that can be migrated in the future to any new players, browsers, or platforms. This protects the intellectual investment in creating the added materials.
- UFM New Media is working closely with glifos.com for integrating this metadata into the library catalog, so as to provide a single point of entry for all materials created on campus.
- In addition to video, glifos.com has developed tools for mounting eBooks. UFM New Media is experimenting with these tools in digitizing rare documents from the library collection and documents of historic interest to the UFM.

Will the creation and use of rich media beget a "disruptive" fusion of content, distribution, and use of materials? It very well might. Christensen devotes a full chapter to discussing how disruptive change should be managed. Under "product development" he mentions three

FIGURE 1. Sample Configuration of the GlifosMedia Player

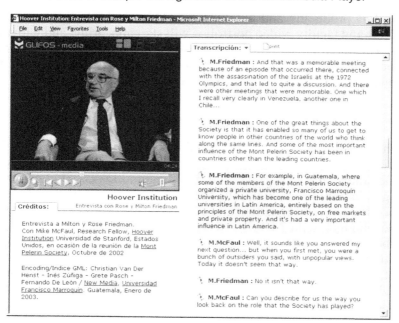

guiding principles, which are adapted as follows for the specific case of the UFM New Media (Christensen, p. 213-215). First, implementing educational content with rich media is *simple, reliable,* and *convenient,* especially for the professor. Second, since XML-based metadata is being used, *changes in function* and *style* can be made quickly and at low cost. And third, one can *hit a low price point.* Even if the upfront investment in enriching the media, per hour, is much higher than simply having a professor teach a class, it's an activity that only needs to be done once and that enables the deployment of an unlimited number of enriched copies of a lecture into the future.

But will rich media disrupt the UFMs traditional educational model? Again, it might. Lectures on video tape are sustaining technologies, and are very boring, because there is no interaction. With streaming videos, students can chat with each other while watching the video. Traditional VHS lectures offer no personalization. Websites can be personalized, why not videos . . . ? And VHS offers little contextual information. Usually, one must simply watch from beginning to end, while with the enriched model one can provide a wealth of paratextual elements that enrich the experience.

And as producing and indexing video becomes more common for students and faculty, video portfolios will start appearing, and with this, an expansion of the current "library collection" into a *digital repository* of local knowledge. The New Media department is helping build the foundations for future information resources.

LESSONS LEARNED

The UFM administration is pleased with the results obtained by New Media. Over 120 hours of fully indexed video are freely accessible on the newmedia.ufm.edu.gt website. Full featured DVDs of conferences and graduation ceremonies have been produced. Rich media-based on-line courses have been taught and evaluated. All this was achieved on a modest budget, with 2 FTEs and 4 part-time personnel.

The administrative strategies that have been successful in implementing the New Media department include creating a separate department, with a separate budget, and a culture where technology can be tested and ideas can thrive. New Media does not create original content, instead, support is provided for academic departments who wish to develop certain materials. New Media suggests which courses and conferences should be recorded and prepared for reuse. Preserving locally produced information and facilitating access to it is one of the main objectives. Since a benefit from the investment in producing media is expected, reusing the materials and distributing them as widely as possible is very important. Long-term thinking for preservation and value of the materials is also important, as is integration of all information resources into a central search location, which is envisioned as an expansion of the library catalog.

The cautious but decisive approach has enabled the UFM to experiment with technologies and services and to invest wisely without falling into costly fads. Pondering the impact of disruptive technologies is also having a deeper impact, by forcing the UFM administration to consider how and if education must change as the result of applying new information technologies and services.

REFERENCES

Arias, Rodrigo and Grete Pasch. 1999. "InfoLib para Web: un sistema de bibliotecas basado en Internet e intranets," *IX Coloquio de Automatización de Bibliotecas*, Universidad de Colima, México. Available at: www.glifos.com/colima1999.html. Date viewed: February 26, 2003.

Baessa, Yetilú and Javier Fernández. 2002. "Comparación de dos Modalidades de Enseñanza del curso de Lógica y Retórica en la Universidad Francisco Marroquín, Guatemala." Available at: www.newmedia.ufm.edu.gt/logica/baessafernandez.pdf. Date viewed: February 26, 2003.

Christensen, Clayton M. 1997. *The Innovator's Dilemma: When New Technologies cause Great Firms to Fail.* Revised and updated edition. Boston, MA: Harvard Business School Press.

Hafner, Katie. 2002. "Lessons Learned at Dot-Com U.," *The New York Times*, May 2, 2002. Available at: www.nytimes.com. Date viewed: May 2, 2002.

Levy, Jonathan D. 2001? *Fusion Education: the Convergence of Virtual Universities.* Available at: www.admin.uio.no/sfa/univett/konferanser/evuforum/Levy.ppt. Date viewed: February 26, 2003.

Pasch, Grete and Rodrigo Arias. 1995. "Sistemas 'a la medida': Desarrollo de InfoLib, un sistema integrado cliente/servidor para bibliotecas," *VII Coloquio de Automatización de Bibliotecas*, Universidad de Colima, México. Available at: www.glifos.com/colima1995.html. Date viewed: February 26, 2003.

Pasch, Grete and Carmen Valdés. 1996. "The Dawn of the Internet Era in Guatemala." In: *Information Technology for Competitiveness in Latin America and the Caribbean.* IFIP 9.4 Conference, Brazil, 1997. Available at: www.nortropic.com/la/ifip.htm. Date viewed: February 24, 2003.

Pasch, Grete and Quinn Stewart. 2002. "Using the Internet to Teach the Internet: An opportunistic Approach," *The Electronic Library*, v.20, no.5: 401-412.

Weller, Martin J. 2001. *Why the Internet is a significant educational technology.* Presented at EDINEB Conference, June 19-22, 2001, Nice, France. Available at: iet.open.ac.uk/pp/m.j.weller/pub/nice.doc. Date viewed: February 24, 2003.

Index

For Product Safety Concerns and Information please contact our EU
representative GPSR@taylorandfrancis.com Taylor & Francis Verlag GmbH,
Kaufingerstraße 24, 80331 München, Germany

Printed and bound by CPI Group (UK) Ltd, Croydon, CR0 4YY
08/06/2025
01896998-0007